LUKE'S PORTRAIT OF JESUS

Bennie Goodwin, Ph.D.

A UMI PUBLICATION

Publisher
Urban Ministries, Inc.
1350 West 103rd Street
Chicago, Illinois 60643
(312) 233-4499

First Edition
First Printing
ISBN: 0-940955-25-3
Catalog No. 9-3000

Copyright © 1993 by Urban Outreach. All rights reserved. No part of this publication may be reproduced, stored in a retrieval system, or transmitted in any form or by any means, electronic, mechanical, photocopy, recording or otherwise except for brief quotations in printed reviews without prior written permission from the holder of the copyright.

Scripture quotations are from *Today's English Version* of the Bible unless otherwise stated. Printed in the United States of America.

DEDICATION

This book is dedicated to my son, Bennie E. Goodwin, III, talented musician and minister.

CONTENTS

AKCNOWLEDGMENTS 8
INTRODUCTION 9

PART I
Understanding Luke

1. Luke, The Writer   15
2. Luke, "The Gospel"   19
3. Freedom: The Central Message   27
4. Major Themes   33

PART II
Luke's Portrait of Jesus

5. Jesus' Heritage and Family   41
6. Jesus: Man With a Following   43
7. Jesus: Man With a Mission   51
8. Jesus: Man of Effective Methods   55
9. Jesus, The Teacher   59

PART III
Jesus, Our Example

10. Experiences: Bethlehem to Nazareth   69
11. Experiences: Galilee to Bethany   79

Notes
Sources and Resources

ACKNOWLEDGMENTS

We wish to acknowledge the outstanding contributions of publications manager and designer, Shawan Brand; copy editor, Mary C. Lewis; cover design, Grant Hoesktra; publications assistants, Caron B. Davis, Geneva K. Ross and Cheryl Wilson; without whose help this book could not have come into existence. Last but not least, we wish to thank Media Graphics Corporation and Dickinson Press, Inc.

INTRODUCTION

Bennie Goodwin, Ph.D.

"The best life of Christ ever written."
"An exceedingly carefully (written) work."
"The Gospel of Gentiles...women...prayer and praise."
"The loveliest book in the world."[1]
"The Gospel of pardon and redemption...sympathy and philanthropy...thanksgiving, singing and joy."[2]
"The most beautiful book ever written."[3]

These are some of the enthusiastic descriptions of people who have read and studied *The Gospel According to St. Luke*. It is our prayer that this book will help you look at the Book of Luke and Jesus, our Saviour and Example, with greater clarity and renewed commitment to love and serve Him.

PERSONAL WORD

In a way, *Luke's Portrait of Jesus* is a tribute to the people of the West End Presbyterian Church and the Cathedral of Faith Church of God in Christ. The author preached sermons from Matthew, Mark, Luke and John at these two churches in Atlanta, Georgia for a total of ten years (1980-1990). For at least two years at each church, sermons were preached only from the Book of Luke. May the Lord continue to reward these congregations for their wonderful patience and encouragement.

Secondly, this book is written as part of a commentary series published by Urban Ministries, Inc., an African American company that for over 22 years continues to produce Christian Education literature and materials for the Black church. May the Lord's richest blessings continue to flow through Dr. Melvin E. Banks, his wife Olive, their children and the staff as they carry on this important ministry.

Luke's Portrait of Jesus

Finally, this book is written with lay persons in mind—especially teachers of Sunday School, Bible School, Vacation Bible School and other non-professional Christian Education workers. We hope this book will be a help and blessing to you as you help prepare Christian leaders for future service.

STRUCTURE

This book is composed of three parts. It begins with a short introductory chapter on the biblical writer, whom we believe to be Luke, and then focuses on the Book of Luke and investigates its purposes, sources, structure, central message and major themes. The second part presents Luke's portrait of Jesus, the book's main character, and explores His heritage, family, following, mission, and methods. Jesus, our Example is the topic of the book's final section. There we look at nine of Jesus' crucial experiences and relate them to some of the experiences we encounter as we "follow in His steps."

HOW TO USE THIS BOOK

1. This book may be used as a teaching supplement or learning enhancement instrument to help you enrich the mental and spiritual lives of your Sunday/church school students—particularly where the lessons are focused in the Book of Luke.

2. You may also use this book as a Sunday School, Bible class or VBS elective course. That is, instead of using your regular adult, young adult or teen curriculum, this book may be used as substitute, or you may ask each student or each family to purchase a copy of this book and use it as a class supplement, research tool or suggested book for additional weekly reading.

3. In addition, this book may be used as part of your personal or family devotions, as a lunchtime Bible study guide at work or as a "Book–of–the–month" selection for a teacher's fellowship at school.

These are a few of the many ways that *Luke's Portrait of Jesus* might be used to enhance knowledge and spiritual growth. You will probably think of other uses as you read and study its content.

Luke's Portrait of Jesus

STYLE

This is not a technically written book. To read this book, you do not need Webster's dictionary in one hand, a Bible dictionary in the other, and commentaries and Bible atlases scattered on your desk or around your feet. It is written simply, clearly and interestingly. It is meant to bless you, not to test your endurance. Read it with excitement in your heart and a prayer on your lips.

HOW TO GET THE MOST OUT OF THIS BOOK

1. First, look at the contents page. Select a chapter that sounds especially interesting to you. Turn to it and read it—just for the pleasure of it.

2. Repeat the process until you've read all of the "special interest" chapters. Then find a *Today's English Version* (TEV) of the Bible, also called *Good News for Modern Man.* Turn to Luke, flip through the chapters and read the stories, incidents and episodes that catch your attention.

3. Come back to this book, begin with Chapter One and read it all the way through, in one setting, if possible.

4. Now go back to the *Good News for Modern Man* version and do the same with the Book of Luke. At this point, you will begin to see Luke as a more organized presentation of Jesus' life and to view Jesus more clearly as a divine-human person. In light of Part Three, you'll probably begin to identify your own Jerusalem, Jordan, Galilee and Transfiguration experiences, and by the time you finish reading this book and Luke through the second time, we wouldn't be surprised if you have fallen in love with the Book of Luke. It may become your favorite "Gospel" or maybe even your favorite book in the Bible.

TODAY'S ENGLISH VERSION (TEV)

As you read through Luke in the *Today's English Version,* you'll recognize it as the version that is quoted most often in this book. We hope this will not offend those of you who normally use only the *King James Version* (KJV). The TEV is probably the simplest, clearest, non-techni-

Luke's Portrait of Jesus

cal version available. It expresses the stories, incidents and episodes in the language many of us use when we preach, teach or write. We revere the old *King James Version*. It's the version we were brought up on; the version from which our mothers and fathers, Sunday School and Vacation Bible teachers taught us to memorize the Scriptures. But we don't speak as King James and his translators did in the 1600s. So please don't reject this book because we used a different version. If you care to, read this book and the TEV along with your *King James Version* and let the total experience build your faith in God and your love for the Lord Jesus Christ.

PART I

UNDERSTANDING LUKE

The word "Luke" refers both to the author and the book more formally called the Gospel According to St. Luke. In this first section, we want to explore Luke the writer, as well as when, where and why he wrote the book that bears his name.

We also want to discuss his book's central message and some of the major themes found there. As you read through this section, we trust that you will not only be informed, but perhaps be inspired as well to record some of your own thoughts and experiences.

1

Luke, The Writer

Isn't it amazing the facts we don't know about things that are so important to us? For instance, we write on paper with pencils and pens. What was the name of the person that invented paper? Pencils? Pens? And what were the dates of their inventions? We don't know, do we? That's something of the condition we find ourselves in when we ask who was the author of the *Gospel According to St. Luke*. When was he born and where? We really don't know. We don't have a record of his birth or the testimony of a person who could say, "I was there" or knew someone who *was* there.

The closest persons we have to Luke are the early church fathers who were the links between Jesus, His disciples and those who lived in the second and third centuries.

1. Date and Place of Birth

An early church source, the *Anti–Marcionite Prologue,* states that Luke was born in Antioch and died, unmarried and childless, in Bocotia at the age of 84.[4] St. Jerome, an early church father called Luke a Syrian, born in Antioch.[5] Again we have to confess, we really don't know precisely when or where Luke was born.

Paul is the first and only New Testament writer to mention Luke. We know from Philemon 23—24 that Timothy worked with Paul, who called him his "fellow worker." And we know that when Paul sent his other assistants to various cities, he would have been all alone, except Luke was with him (2 Timothy 4:9-11).

Luke's Portrait of Jesus

2. Paul's Traveling Companion

Other evidence of a connection between Paul and Luke are the so-called "we" passages. It is believed that Luke also wrote *The Acts of the Apostles*. In at least three places in Acts the writer slips into first person plural. Instead of saying "they," he says "we" (Acts 16:10-17; 20:5--21:18; 27:1--28:16). If, as we believe, the author of both Luke and Acts is Luke, then Luke was with Paul in Philippi (Acts 16:10-17), Troas (20:5-6), Mitylene (20:14), Samos and Miletus (20:15), Cos, Rhodes, Patara (21:1), Tyre (21:3), Ptolemais (21:7), Ceasarea (21:8-16) and Jerusalem (21:17-18).

The final "we" passage puts Paul, Aristarchus and Luke together on their way to Rome (27:1-2). They arrived there after sailing by way of Sidon (27:3), Myra, (27:5), Crete (27:7), Malta (also called Melita, 28:1), Syracuse (28:12) and Puteoli, an Italian port (28:13).[6]

3. A Medical Doctor

Paul's letter to the Colossians reveals that Luke was a doctor, "a beloved physician" (Colossians 4:14). The Muratorian Canon, an early church document, also calls Luke a physician who wrote the Gospel of Luke and the Book of Acts.[7] Earlier Bible scholars thought they detected special medical language in Luke's writing. After more research, it was suggested that Luke's language was not special but "that the language used in Luke–Acts to describe ailments and cures *is* compatible with the ancient tradition that the author was a doctor."[8]

4. A Gentile

It is believed by some writers that Luke was also a Gentile and therefore the only non–Jewish writer of a New Testament book. This belief is based on Colossians 4:10 and 4:14. There Paul first sends greetings from his Jewish assistants, calling them "of the circumcision" (4:11). Then he speaks of Luke and Demas whom it may be assumed are Gentiles and not "of the circumcision" (4:14). Other scholars point to Luke's special interest in Gentiles in both Luke and Acts and his fluency in the Greek language.[9] Commentator Albert Barnes confirmed that

Luke, The Writer

although Luke was "intimately acquainted with Jewish rites, customs, opinions and prejudices," he was a Jewish–Christian *convert* 'born of Gentile parents.'"[10]

5. Compassionate

One of the qualities that comes through in Luke's writing is his social consciousness and his "inexhaustible sympathy for the troubles of other people."[11] His story of Jesus is sometimes called the "Gospel of the underdog."[12] Whether the victim is a woman, a child, a tax collector or a Samaritan, Luke is interested and sympathetic. He presents Jesus and the apostles as concerned servants of the sick, the helpless and hopeless. He has an eye for the hurting and a heart for their needs.

6. Historian

Howard Marshall has said in *Luke: Historian and Theologian*, "the task of the historian is to reconstruct the past, to give an account of events as they actually happened."[13] That is what Luke sets out to do.

Luke was not an eyewitness disciple, so he had to do what many historians are required to do. He had to conduct research. He said in his introduction, "I have carefully studied all these matters from their beginning" in order to "write an orderly account..." (Luke 1:3, TEV). He did such an outstanding job that his Gospel account has been called "the best life of Christ ever written," and a "product of the most careful historical research."[14] He probably interviewed many people, including Jesus' mother, and if the "we" passages were written by Luke, he surely knew Peter and James (Acts 15:13-14). And it's not hard to imagine the doctor going around the Jerusalem Council meetings with scroll in hand, asking questions, gathering and confirming information for his books.

7. Theologian   *careful study of the facts*

Luke was not only interested in the facts, he was also interested in the meaning of the facts. He promised Theophilus an "orderly account" but also the "full truth" (Luke 1:4). That meant Luke had to interpret the

Luke's Portrait of Jesus

facts. He had to select the facts and events and put them together so that Jesus' ministry of healing, help and hope could be clearly perceived and received. He was not only interested in what happened but in why it happened and what the results were. Luke not only records that Jesus' ascended into heaven *but also* that the disciples worshiped Him and went back into Jerusalem, filled with great joy. There they spent their time in the temple, giving thanks to God (24:50-53). Through Luke's selection of facts and events, he disclosed their meaning.

8. Storyteller *Just the Facts!*

Luke's basic theological method was storytelling. Seldom is Luke's voice heard. He recounts his history and does his interpretation through the voices of others. Nowhere does he call Jesus' birth the "Virgin Birth". He simply tells of the conversation between an angel and a virgin and records the outcome (1:26-38). Nowhere does he discuss the doctrine of divine "faith" healing. He simply tells story after story of miraculous healing. Nowhere does he discuss demonology. He just shows Jesus healing "Mr. Legion" (8:26-40) and casting out demons, in the synagogue and on Peter's mother–in–law's porch. Nowhere does he expound the doctrine of forgiveness—even last–minute, death–bed salvation. He records that Jesus forgave a sinner while on the Cross and promised to take a dying thief into Paradise (23:39-43).

Even though we don't know when or where Luke was born, we thank God for anointing this compassionate Gentile physician who gave the Church and the world accurate history and superb Christian theology in stories.

2

Luke, "The Gospel"

Why did Luke write this book? Where did he get his information? When did he write it and where was he when he wrote it? What is the structure, content, central message and major theme of his book, and what is Luke's unique contribution to our knowledge of Jesus' life and ministry? These are some of the questions that we will attempt to answer in this section.

1. Purpose

First let's talk about why Luke wrote the book that has been given his name. After all, we believe that Mark and Matthew had already written their Gospel accounts. Why did Luke feel another Gospel account was needed? From Luke's prologue (1:1-4), we glean that he wrote because *he wanted to*. He had taken the time and effort to gather information from various sources, to study it carefully and organize it diligently. After having done all that work he wanted to complete the process, by writing it and sharing it with other persons.

A second reason he wrote his book is because he felt *he needed to*. It is usually agreed that Matthew's account is meant primarily for the Jews. It has many quotes from the Old Testament with which the Jews were familiar. Matthew repeats the phrase, "that it might fulfilled" to show that Jesus is the Person that many Old Testament persons said would come. On the other hand, Mark's account is intended primarily for the practical minded Romans. There is no genealogy in Mark. The Romans were not very much concerned about where people came from. Their concern was what a person could do, produce or contribute. So in

Luke's Portrait of Jesus

Mark the words "straightway" and "immediately" are prominent. Jesus is shown as a Man of action. Mark uses a one–verse introduction and before the first chapter of Mark is complete, Jesus is recorded as having already cast out demons and healed many sick people.

We believe Luke read Matthew and Mark and felt that another view of Jesus was needed, a view that was especially appealing to the Greeks. Therefore, he wrote his Gospel account and addressed it to a Grecian or at least a man with a Greek name called Theophilus. We're not sure who Theophilus was, but his name means "beloved of God" and it is believed that since Luke addressed him as "most excellent," he was a high ranking official in the Roman government.[15]

A third reason that Luke wrote is theological. Not only did Luke want and need to write, in a sense *he had to* write. As a Christian, committed to doing God's will, we believe he was moved, urged and inspired by the Lord to write an orderly account of what he had discovered.

Paul talked about being constrained by the love of Christ (2 Corinthians 5:14, KJV) and said, "Woe is unto me, if I preach not the gospel!" (1 Corinthians 9:16, KJV) He told Timothy that all Scripture was inspired by God and is useful for "teaching...rebuking...correcting...and giving instruction for right living" (2 Timothy 3:16, TEV). Could Luke have chosen not to write his account? Yes, we suppose he could have. But oh, how much poorer he and we would have been. In the sense that Moses *had to* go to Egypt and Jeremiah *had to* prophesy; in the sense that Mahalia Jackson *had to* sing and George Washington Carver *had to* discover and invent; in that sense, Luke *had to* write. God gave him the talent, he saw the need and wanted to fulfill it. So he wrote his Gospel account because he wanted to, needed to and had to.

2. Sources

Luke was not one of the disciples. He did not travel with Jesus like Matthew and John. Then where did he get the information to write the book called by his name? Well, there seemed to be four main sources. First is Mark's account. Most scholars agree that about 350 of Luke's 661 verses are taken directly from Mark. A second source is Matthew, which accounts for 325 verses of Luke's information. And then there is a

Luke, "The Gospel"

source called "Q" which is the first letter of the word *Quelle* which simply means "source." *Q* is thought to be a written document that contained various sayings of Jesus which were copied down by people who heard Jesus speak and wanted to remember what He said. Finally, Luke added various stories and incidents that are unique to his account and that he probably gathered from personal interviews.[16] For instance, who could have possibly told him about Jesus' birth except Mary or Joseph?

So, what were the sources of Luke's material? Mark, Matthew, *Q* and the results of Luke's own research. Luke's source–formula might look like this:

Mark + Matthew + Q + Luke's personal research = Luke's Gospel account.

Someone has also noted that Luke spent time with Paul and some of the other disciples, and that the preaching of these apostles gave him additional information and influenced his perspective.[17]

3. Date and Place

We really do not know when and where Luke wrote his account. Various scholars have suggested dates as early as 60 A.D. and as late as 90 A.D.[18] We simply do not know, but a safe guess seems to be around 63 A.D., about 30 years after Jesus' death, resurrection and ascension and about seven or eight years before the capture of Jerusalem, which Luke mentions as a prophecy (21:20-24) but not as having already taken place.

The place of Luke's writing is even more uncertain. Rome, Ephesus, Antioch have been suggested, as well as Corinth, Bithynia, Caesarea in Palestine and Alexandra in Egypt.[19] In all honesty, we'll have to say we don't know, and the possibilities are so numerous that we can't even make an educated guess.

4. Structure

In his introduction (1:1-4) Luke told Theophilus that he had written him an orderly account (1:3). What is Luke's order? Perhaps the simplest way to describe Luke's structure is Jesus' birth, ministry, death, resurrection and ascension. That is the essential structure—the beginning,

Luke's Portrait of Jesus

middle and the end. But to help us get a better perspective, let's use this outline as our basic framework:

I. 1:1-4: Introduction
II. 1:5--4:13: Jesus' Birth and Preparation for Ministry
III. 4:14--21:38: Jesus' Public Ministry
IV. 22:1--24:53: Jesus' Last Days on Earth

Now let's fill in these four main sections with a little more detail.

I. Introduction (1:1-4)

II. Jesus' Birth and Preparation for Ministry (1:5--4:13)
    A. The Birth of John and Jesus (1:5--2:21)
    B. The Infancy and Boyhood of Jesus (2:22-52)
    C. The Preaching of John the Baptist (3:1-20)
    D. The Baptism, Ancestors and Temptation of Jesus (3:21--4:13)

III. Jesus' Public Ministry (4:14--21:38)
    A. Ministry in Galilee (4:14--9:50)
    B. Ministry on the Way to Jerusalem (9:51--19:27)
    C. Ministry in Jerusalem (19:28--21:38)

IV. Jesus' Last Days on Earth (22:1--24:53)
    A. The Lord's Supper (22:1-38)
    B. The Arrest and Trial (22:39--23:25)
    C. The Crucifixion (23:26-56)
    D. The Resurrection and Ascension (24:1-53)

5. Summary of Content
I. Introduction (1:1-4) In the introduction, Luke gives us information about: a) to whom his book is addressed (1:1), b) the general sources of his information (1:2), c) the method he used to prepare the manuscript

Luke, "The Gospel"

and d) the reasons he wrote his book (1:4). Luke's book is the only one of the Gospel accounts to include such information.

II. Jesus' Birth and Preparation for Ministry (1:5--4:13) In the second section of Luke's "Gospel," he tells about John the Baptist—his parents, birth and preaching (a sample sermon). In this section he also tells us of Jesus' birth, his parents and the visits of the shepherds and angels. In addition, he informs us about Jesus' first trip to the temple in Jerusalem and about the reception He received from Simeon and Anna. Here we also learn about Jesus' boyhood, baptism and His ancestors, dating all the way back to Adam. Luke concludes this second section by giving us a glimpse of Jesus' wilderness experience. These experiences helped prepare Jesus for His exciting and challenging ministry.

III. Jesus' Public Ministry (4:14--21:38) Jesus' public ministry comprises the largest section of Luke's Gospel and includes His ministry in Galilee, where He experiences rejection in Nazareth, His hometown but popularity in other parts of Galilee—particularly Capernaum. Then Luke gives much detail about what Jesus did and said on His way to Jerusalem. Luke uses almost ten chapters (9:51--19:27) to describe Jesus' trip and includes much material from his primary sources. This section contains some of Jesus' most interesting and memorable stories—the good Samaritan, the prodigal son, and the story of the rich man and Lazarus. If this was the only section of Luke we had, it would be well worth reading and preserving. Luke concludes this part of his account by telling us what happened when Jesus arrived in Jerusalem and began to minister there.

IV. Jesus' Last Days on Earth (22:1--24:53) Luke brings his book to a dramatic close with his account of Jesus' final days on earth. The first Lord's Supper, His battle and surrender in Gethsemane, Judas' betrayal, Jesus' trial, arrest and crucifixion are all very sad experiences for a Person who has spent His entire life "doing good" (Acts 10:38). But in harmony with the other Gospel writers, Luke assures us that the story does not end on Good Friday. For the book to be a Gospel there must be "good news." Humanity had done its worst but humanity did not have the last words. The last words are good words. They are words that describe God's action. The words are "Resurrection" and "Ascension."

> Because He lives
> I can face tomorrow;
> Because He lives
> All fear is gone;
> Because I know
> He holds the future,
> Life is worth the living
> Just because He lives.[20]

That's Good News. That's how Luke ends his Gospel account. How else could he end it? It's the Gospel of Jesus Christ!

6. Luke's Unique Content

One of the reasons Luke wrote his account was to tell Theophilus the "full truth" about what he had been taught about Jesus. Luke had "dug up" some information that had not been recorded by Mark or Matthew. He felt it was important that the facts he had discovered be written down in an orderly fashion. What was this information?

It was information about Zechariah and Elizabeth, the parents of John the Baptist. How would we have known that John's father was a priest or that John was not born until his parents were "up in age?" John was a miracle child and like Samuel, he was born in answer to prayer. How would we have known that Mary and Zechariah could sing (Luke 1:46-55, 67-79), and that John was under the full control of the Holy Spirit even before he was born? (1:15) How would we have known that John and Jesus were cousins and might have known each other *before* they met at Jordan? (1:36)

Matthew told us that Jesus was born in Bethlehem (1:18-25), but how would we have known about the angelic chorus and the shepherds

Luke, "The Gospel"

who came to celebrate Jesus' birth? How would we have known about Simeon and Anna in the temple, and that Jesus was content to stay there in His "Father's place of business" but obeyed His parents and went back home where He developed in mind, body and spirit? We couldn't have known about all these things except by reading Luke. Now, we will not talk about each unique piece of information that Luke gives us. But for those who want the information and experience of the "L" source (original Luke material), here are some suggestions: 1. Read the verses that follow this paragraph. 2. Read Luke's account in the *Today's English Version* (TEV). There the stories and passages are separated into smaller individual units, so that the content of the passages stands out. And under the title of each passage, it tells whether the same passage is found in one of the other Gospel accounts.

Here are Luke's unique scriptural passages:

1:1-80	14:7-14
2:8-52	15:8-10
7:11-17, 36-50	15:11-32
8:1-3	16:1-18
9:51-56	16:19-31
10:1-12	17:5-6
10:17-20	17:7-10
10:25-37	17:11-19
10:38-42	18:1-8
11:27-28	18:9-14
12:13-21	19:1-10
12:35-40	19:41-44
13:1-5	22:24-30
13:6-9	22:35-38
13:10-17	23:6-12
14:1-6	24:13-35

3

Freedom: The Central Message

God is present in Jesus to free us from the power of **Sin, Sickness, Fear, Demons and Death.** Luke is not a preacher; therefore, he does not hammer that message home to us as Paul or John does in their letters, or as Peter does in his sermons. Luke is a writer–dramatist, and he conveys his central message in story form through the voices of his characters.

1. God Is Present in Jesus

Through Zechariah, Luke links his message to the Jewish prophets, priests and kings of the Old Testament. Beginning in verse 5, Luke acknowledges the presence of God by writing that both Zechariah and Elizabeth "lived good lives in God's sight and obeyed fully all the Lord's laws and commandments." From that verse to the last verse of chapter 24—where in verse 53 the disciples are said to have "spent all their time in the Temple giving thanks to God"—you'll find Luke's book to be saturated with the consciousness that God is present through Jesus and in the lives of those who trust Him.

2. God Is Present to Free Us From Sin

The reason for God's presence is our freedom. Ever since Adam and Eve sinned in the Garden of Eden, we have experienced bondage. Satan didn't tell us that along with the knowledge of good and evil came the bondage of evil. Isn't Zechariah's dilemma an illustration of this? He's a priest. He knows an angel when he sees one. He knows that the angel's words are God's words, but he is not free to believe the angel.

Luke's Portrait of Jesus

Isn't this also illustrated by Jesus' rejection by His home folk? They listen to the voice of God through Scripture, they have heard of the miracles the Lord has performed through Jesus. They know that He represents the presence and power of God, but they are not free to accept Him. They are bound by the sin of prejudice and decide it is easier to get rid of Jesus than it is to get rid of their prejudice.

By contrast, "Brother Paralee" (5:17-26), "Sister Forgiven" (7:36-50) and "Brother Zack" (19:1-10) not only know the bondage of their sins but also they recognize and trust the power of God present in Jesus. They go from His presence forgiven, set free, made whole.

3. God Is Present to Free Us From Sickness

Luke presents many examples of Jesus setting people free from sickness. Three of the most dramatic examples are "Brother Lep" (5:11-16), "Brother Witherly" (6:6-11) and "Sister Persistence" (8:43-48). How could anyone read Luke's thrilling episodes and miss his point—that God is present in Jesus to free us from the bondage of sickness. Does God heal everybody? No. Can God heal everybody? Yes. Is it possible to be sick and yet not *bound* by sickness? Yes. Ask Paul; that was exactly the point he made in 2 Corinthians 12:7-9. Is it possible to escape the presence of sin and sickness? Not in this world. Is it possible to experience victory over either? Yes, by the power of God in Jesus Christ.

4. God Is Present to Free Us From Fear

As we read Luke's book, one of the phrases that keeps confronting us is, "fear not" (KJV) or "don't be afraid" (TEV). Those were the angel's first words to Zechariah (1:13), his second words to Mary (1:30), and his first words to the shepherds (2:10). Those were Jesus' words to His first four frightened disciples (5:10) and the words he used to calm the fears of Jarius (8:50). Luke does not tell us, but Matthew does, that the first angels' words to the women who came to the tomb on Easter morning were, "fear not" and Jesus' second words to the frightened sisters were, "Do not be afraid" (Matthew 28:10).

Freedom: The Central Message

What is the message? God is present to free us from fear—fear that our yesterdays will catch up with us and intrude on our todays; fear that today's strength will not be adequate for tomorrow; fear that our physical, mental or moral resources will not be able to sustain us "for the long haul;" fear that our financial ends will not continue to meet; fear that we will be betrayed or abandoned by our loved ones. Fear, Fear, FEAR.

We feel these fears and countless others but dare not mention them—lest they reach up from a bottomless abyss and drag us down. It is to these fears that God speaks: "Fear not, do not be afraid." The poet captures these liberating words from Isaiah 43 and puts them to song:[21]

> Fear not, I am with thee,
> O be not dismayed,
> For I am thy God,
> And will still give thee aid;
> I'll strengthen thee, help thee,
> And cause thee to stand,
> Upheld by my righteous,
> Omnipotent hand.[22]

Through Jesus Christ, we respond with words from an Old Testament hymn writer:

> "I will fear no evil:
> for thou art with me…"
> (Psalm 23:4, KJV).

> "God is our refuge and strength,
> a very present help in trouble.
> Therefore we will not fear…"
> (Psalm 46:1-2a, KJV).

Luke's Portrait of Jesus

5. God Is Present to Free Us From the Power of Demons

Are demons real? Are there spiritual creatures who are committed to evil and live under the control of Satan? In the context of the New Testament, these are purely academic questions, and ones to which all of the New Testament writers and Jesus give a resounding, unequivocal yes!

Ask the man in the Capernaum synagogue (Luke 4:31-36) or "Mr. Legion" in the Gerasa graveyard (8:26-39). Interview the father at the foot of Transfiguration Mountain (9:37-43), or the lady who became "Sister Bentover" (13:10-17). Ask any of them and they will tell you that demons are real. They will also tell you that in Jesus, they discovered that God was present to free them from the power of these demons.

Now, in addition to these evil spiritual personalities, there exists for each of us that which cannot necessarily be "blamed on" a specific evil person. Is it accurate to say that there is something demonic in human nature itself? Something contrary, something opposite to that which is good and positive? Something that won't let us enjoy the good, the true and beautiful in life but for a short time before it interrupts. This perversity seems almost inherent in life itself. It is that insistent something in the back of our minds which tells us when things are going well to watch out, because it's "too good to be true." And sure enough, in a little while something perverse happens.

And then there are demonic habits—such as alcoholism, drug addiction, sexual promiscuity, pernicious materialism, lying, stealing and gossiping—that grab us by our moral throats and will not let us go. Add to these the awful, denigrating, destructive relationships that we are sucked into, and like quicksand in slow motion, they gradually carry us down until we cry like Peter, "Save me, Lord!" (Matthew 14:30) The Good News of Luke (and all the other New Testament writers) is that God is present to free us from the power of our demons, no matter what they may be. As the song from *O for a Thousand Tongues to Sing* reminds us, "He breaks the power of canceled sin and sets the prisoner free." That is an important part of Luke's central message.

Freedom: The Central Message

6. God Is Present to Free Us From the Power of Death

Does this mean that those who respond in faith to God through Jesus Christ will not die? On the physical level, the answer is no. Even for persons like "Brother Nain" (Luke 17:11-17) and "Little Sister Jarius" (8:49-56), as far as we know the extension of their physical life was temporary. Jesus brought them back to life but as far as we know, they along with Lazarus (John 11:1-44) died again.

Luke was trying to have us understand that their resurrection, though temporary, was a symbol of what the presence of God can do. Just as Jesus raised Brother Nain and Sister Jarius from physical death and gave them back to their parents, God is present to give spiritual life to all who will accept it. Isn't this the real lesson of Luke's resurrection stories? Isn't this the basic, underlying lesson of Jesus' resurrection? It's a display of God's power. Did Luke discover that principle himself, or did he hear it as a traveling companion to Paul? Was he with Paul when he wrote as a prisoner in Rome, "All I want is to know Christ and to experience the power of his resurrection..." (Philippians 3:10, TEV).

Luke included his dramatic resurrection stories to assure his original readers and us that God is present in Jesus Christ to free us from the power of death—from the power that physical death has over us and from the experience of spiritual death. Hear John as he adds, "If the Son therefore shall make you free,... [you] shall be free indeed" (John 8:36, KJV). Yes, Jesus Christ came to free us from the power of sin, sickness, fear, demons and death. That is Luke's central message.

4

Major Themes

If Luke's central message is that God is present to free us from the power of sin, sickness, fear, demons and death, what are some his major themes?

1. Freedom for Gentiles

One of Luke's major themes is that God extends freedom to Gentiles as well as Jews.[23] Some of the children of Abraham misunderstood God's reason for their chosenness. They seemed to have thought that God chose them to be His **exclusive** people. In reality, God told Abraham right from the beginning and reiterated it to Isaac and Jacob that through the Jews all the nations of the earth were to be blessed (Genesis 12:3).

The people of Nazareth didn't understand that, or understood it and refused to accept it. So when Jesus started talking about bringing Good News to the Gentile poor, setting Gentile captives free and the Lord saving Gentile people, they dragged their most famous citizen out of town and would have thrown Him off a cliff if He hadn't walked away (Luke 4:18-19, 28-29). Luke wrote his book to emphasize that everybody, even despised Samaritans are included in God's plan of freedom (7:1-19; 10:25-37; 17:11-19; 23:47).

Simeon understood this emphasis well and reflected it in his prayer:

"Now, Lord, you have kept your promise, and you may let your servant go in peace. With my own eyes I have seen your salvation, which you have prepared in the presence of all peoples: A light to reveal your will to the Gentiles and bring glory to your people Israel" (2:29-32).

Luke's Portrait of Jesus

2. Freedom for the Poor

Luke began his book by telling us that Jesus came from a poor family. Not only is this illustrated by the fact that Jesus was born in a stable, laid in a cattle trough and covered with a coarse cloth (2:7), but His first guests were poor shepherds (2:8-20), and His poor parents could only provide the minimum sacrifice for His dedication (2:22-24). In Mary's song are references to the lowly and hungry (1:48, 52-53), and when the people asked John the Baptist what they should do to show their sincere repentance, he told them to share one of their shirts with a poor person who had none (3:11).

Jesus declared that one of His prophetic missions was "to bring good news to the poor" (4:18, TEV). A person's economic status was never a basis for refusal when that person looked to Jesus for help, and when John sent for a confirmation from Jesus that He was the real Messiah, Jesus told John's messengers to tell him that "the Good News is preached to the poor" (7:22, TEV).

Lazarus was so poor he literally starved to death but he was welcomed into Abraham's bosom. He was too poor to live on earth but he was just right for heaven! (16:19-31) Jesus sent disciples out to minister as poor men. He told them to take nothing extra and to be sustained by those to whom they ministered (10:1-8). Perhaps we cannot say that Jesus is against rich people, but Luke definitely shows that He is *for* poor people. He told the disciples that the poor were "blessed" or "happy," not because they were poor but because the kingdom of God belonged to them! (6:20)

3. Freedom for Women

It is probably not by chance that Luke introduces three women (Elizabeth, Mary and Anna) in the first two chapters of his Gospel. Twelve verses are devoted to the angel's conversation with Mary (1:26-38), and another 17 verses are given to Elizabeth's conversation with Mary and her song of praise (1:39-56). In chapter seven, Jesus raises a poor widow's only son back to life (7:11-17) and frees the town prostitute from a life of sin (7:36-60). In chapter eight Luke informs us that

Major Themes

Jesus had women disciples who traveled with Him to various towns and villages, ministering with Him and to Him (8:1-3). Later in the same chapter, a lady is healed of a blood disease just by touching His robe and He heals a little girl that everybody, except Jesus, said was dead (8:40-42, 49-56).

Two of Jesus' favorite people were Mary and Martha. A little incident in their home is mentioned in chapter 10, verses 38-42 (see also John 11:1-44). And in chapter 13 Luke tells the story of "Sister Bentover" who suffered with a problem for 18 years. Jesus freed her from her "spirit of infirmity" and made her "Sister Straight" (13:10-17, KJV). In Luke's trilogy of lost and found stories, he included one about a woman who lost one of her silver coins. When she found it, she "threw a party" to celebrate. Jesus said that's what happens in heaven when one sinner experiences spiritual freedom (15:8-10).

One of Jesus' most well-known stories is found in chapter 18. It's about a woman who gave a judge no rest until he gave her justice. This is a story of contrast. Jesus said that people won't have to treat God like this lady treated the unjust judge. He said, "I tell you [God] will judge in [your] favor and do it quickly" (18:8). In chapter 21, Jesus used the poor widow who gave two copper coins as a demonstration of generosity. Jesus said she out-gave all of the rich contributors because she "gave all she had to live on" (21:1-4).

Luke noted in chapter 22 that it was a young woman who first recognized Peter as one of Jesus' disciples. His denial finally led to tears of embarrassment and repentance (22:54-62). In the following chapter Luke records a brief conversation between some woman and Jesus as He was on His way to be crucified. They were weeping and wailing because they knew Jesus did not deserve the torture He was about to endure. Instead of joining the "pity party," Jesus encouraged them to refocus their concern on themselves and their children, in anticipation of the terrible days that were ahead for the people who lived in Jerusalem. Those who were alive in 70 A.D. when Jerusalem was destroyed, understood the experience His vivid words described (23:27-31).

After Jesus' death some of the women who had come with Him to Jerusalem from Galilee went with Joseph of Arimathea to bury Him.

Luke's Portrait of Jesus

They were the first persons at the tomb on Easter Sunday morning, where they found the giant stone rolled away and heard the angel's words: "He is not here!" They carried the news back to Jesus' frightened and unbelieving disciples (Luke 24:1-11). And Luke was careful to mention in his second book, *The Acts of the Apostles,* that women were present in the Upper Room when the Spirit arrived (Luke 23:55-56; 24:1-11; Acts 1:14). It is said that the daily prayer of many Jewish men in Jesus' day included the phrase, Thank God that you didn't make me a "Gentile, a slave or a woman."[24] Do you think Luke or Jesus prayed such a prayer?

Why did Luke choose stories and incidents that include at least 20 women and in some way connects them to Jesus? What is Luke trying to tell us about Jesus? Or, what is God trying to tell us through Jesus about His attitude toward women? I think Luke reminds us of at least three principles:

1. Women have serious physical, mental, emotional, social and spiritual problems just as men do, and they need to experience the freedom that God gives to women *and* men through Jesus Christ.

2. Women have qualities such as love, persistence, dependability, endurance, generosity, perceptivity and commitment that God appreciates.

3. Women are welcome in the ministry of Jesus. Here they can share their gifts, talents, abilities, experiences and skills to the glory of God and the good of people.

4. Freedom to Serve

A. God's Servants—Service to God and people is one of the major themes that runs through Luke's Gospel. In the first few verses of chapter one we meet Zechariah as he serves God in the temple (1:8). In Mary's song, she speaks of herself as God's lowly servant (1:48) and in Zechariah's prophecy, he remembers how God promised to free Israel from her enemies so that they could "serve Him without fear" (1:73-74). In Simeon's prayer of gratitude, he speaks of himself as God's servant and when Jesus resists Satan's temptations, He quotes the Scripture that God alone is to be worshiped and served (4:8). So even in the first four chapters, Luke sets the stage for Jesus' emphasis on service.

Major Themes

B. Called and Chosen—Now you might think that since Jesus was so talented, gifted, anointed and focused, He would carry on His ministry alone. After all, He can do anything that needs to be done. He can heal, cast out demons, preach, teach and even forgive sin. What more does He need? He needs some help and almost immediately goes out to recruit some helpers, learners, and disciples. He finds the first four out fishing in the Sea of Galilee. He encourages them by helping them catch more fish than they have ever caught before and then calls them to leave the fishing business and follow Him. Amazingly enough, they pull their boats onto the beach, leave everything and follow Him (5:1-11). Sometime later He found Matthew (Levi), the "IRS man" and recruited him (5:27-32). By chapter 6, verses 12-16, He has His full number.

C. Prepared and Sent—The diverse group listed, constitute the 12 men who will be His closest associates. He will tell them His kingdom principles (6:17-49; also see Matthew 5:1—7:28), demonstrate kingdom power (Luke 7:1—9:43) and send them out to do kingdom business (9:1-6). Others will join them (8:1-3; 10:1-12), but of these 12, 11 will constitute the nucleus whom Jesus will send to teach and preach the Good News to the whole world (24:47; Matthew 28:18-20; Mark 16:15-19; Acts 1:8).

D. The Discipleship Principle—Why did Jesus bother selecting and preparing such a motley group as the disciples were before Pentecost? Why did He invest so much time and thought, energy and prayer in them? They were often "slow" of mind and heart (Luke 8:9-10, 24-25; 9:12-14, 37-40, 45; 18:31-34) and at times seemed much more interested in their own agendas (9:46-48; 22:24-30). Sometimes they doubted their own senses (24:36-42). But Jesus kept working with them because He knew this principle: Our most effective and lasting ministry will not be done by ourselves, but by those whom we influence. There are over one billion Christians in the world today,[25] because Jesus took the time and patience to call, choose, prepare and send forth disciples and give them the power and freedom to serve.

Luke's Portrait of Jesus

5. SUMMARY
These then are Luke's four major themes:
1. Freedom for Gentiles
2. Freedom for the poor
3. Freedom for women
4. Freedom to serve

PART II

LUKE'S PORTRAIT OF JESUS

It is rumored that Luke was an artist and painted a picture of Jesus' mother that is still in existence.[26] We cannot prove that the rumor is true, but in Luke's Gospel we have a beautiful word portrait of Jesus to observe and admire. Luke's book has been called "the loveliest book in the world" and "the best life of Christ ever written."[27] Let's discover how Luke "painted" his picture of Christ.

One of the first things we notice is that, other than the Introduction (1:1-4), Luke does not speak in his own voice, but instead allows his characters to use their voices and therefore add their own brush strokes to the painting. His portrait of Christ has lots of color as persons tell their stories in their own words. Luke provides the background that blends the colors together by citing historical facts and inserting transitions. Luke's portrait of Jesus is painted by contributions from saints like Simeon and Anna, Jesus' parents and Jewish leaders, the disciples and civil leaders like Herod and Pilate, angels and demons, Satan and Gabriel, individuals and crowds, the sick and those who cared for them, the good and bad, the beautiful and ugly.

On many occasions we hear Jesus' own words and on rare occasions God speaks—but only to Jesus. Luke's portrait is bright and rich, dark and foreboding. Come along as we "see Jesus" (John 12:21). You may not always like what you see, but in no case will you be bored.

5

Jesus' Heritage and Family

1. Jesus: Man With a Heritage

Luke begins his Gospel account by demonstrating that Jesus didn't just appear out of nowhere like Melchizedek, Elijah or Joel. No, Jesus had a heritage; a human heritage, a Jewish heritage and a divine heritage. Luke links Jesus with John the Baptist, whose father Zechariah was a Jewish priest and whose mother also belonged to the tribe of Levi—one of Jacob's sons (1:5). To tighten the Jewish heritage more securely, Luke notes that John the Baptist and Jesus were relatives because Elizabeth and Mary, Jesus' mother are related (1:36). To further cement Jesus' Jewishness and to emphasis His human heritage, Luke includes a family tree that extends all the way back to Adam (3:23-38).

But Luke wants to make sure we understand that Jesus is not just human, so he adds this phrase to the genealogy, "the son of God" (3:38). In case we might miss that little phrase hanging on the end of a long genealogy that not many contemporary people read, he reports that the angel said to Mary, "The Holy Spirit will come on you, and God's power will rest upon you. For this reason the holy child will be called the Son of God" (1:35, TEV).

Later when God speaks in His own voice, He confirms the words of Gabriel. At Jesus' baptism (3:21-22) and at His transfiguration experience (9:35), God affirms Jesus as His Son. Luke impresses upon us that Jesus is a man with a heritage—human, Jewish and divine.

2. Jesus: Man With a Family

Jesus was blessed with a mom and stepfather. They brought Him into

Luke's Portrait of Jesus

the world, helped Him survive those first few uncomfortable days in a Bethlehem stable, showed Him off to the shepherds, had Him circumcised and gave Him a name (2:1-22). They took Him to the temple where Zechariah had met the angel while carrying out his priestly duties. There He was blessed by Simeon and Anna (2:27-32) who were sure that He was the Messiah they had been waiting to see.

Later His mom and stepfather took Him back to the temple where they inadvertently left Him. They were very upset when they couldn't find Him and had to go all the way back to Jerusalem to locate Him. Just as they probably suspected, as an intelligent young man of 12, He was in the temple conversing "with the Jewish teachers" (2:46). His mom gave Him a verbal spanking and like a good boy, He went on back to Nazareth where He matured physically, mentally, spiritually and socially (2:41-52). After the temple episode we don't hear any more about His stepfather, Joseph. Perhaps he died early. But he must have been a good model—so good that Jesus adopted "father" as the primary symbol of His close relationship with God.

Jesus had at least four brothers (James, Joseph, Judas and Simon) and several sisters (Mark 6:3) whom Luke does not tell us about. But Luke does tell us that his mother and brothers sometimes visited Him while He was ministering (8:19-21). When He was crucified and buried, His mother was there (John 19:25), and she was present, along with some of Jesus' brothers, when the disciples met in the "Upper Room" after Jesus' ascension (Acts 1:14). Luke tells us in the Book of Acts that two of Jesus' brothers, James and Judas (Jude) became prominent leaders in the early church. James became the leader of the church and Jude wrote the little New Testament book that bears his name. Jesus came from a good, strong family. They were not rich materially but under the leadership of Joseph and Mary, they developed into a strong spiritual unit that nurtured Jesus and helped other family members to find their places and make positive contributions.

6

Jesus: Man With a Following

> Are you a leader?
> Look behind you
> If no one is following you
> You're not a leader;
> You're just out taking a walk![28]

1. A Popular Leader

After Jesus' time of temptation in the wilderness (4:1-13) and rejection in Nazareth (4:16-30), He became a very popular leader—especially in the area of Galilee. He taught, preached and healed in the synagogues, in homes and in the open air. He was so much in demand until after sunset (4:40) and before sunrise, people were looking for Him "by the droves." They sometimes "tried to keeping him from leaving" a particular place and He had to break away and go on to the next area anyhow (4:42). Once He had to get into a boat and push away from the shore in order to keep from getting mobbed and possibly pushed into the water as He taught (5:1-3; Matthew 4:25). At another time, 5,000 men, plus women and children, possibly 15,000 people, stayed all day, watching Him heal and listening to His fascinating words. Jesus and His disciples had tried to get away, and the people saw them and intercepted them by running to beat their boat to shore. They were so excited about the miracle of the two fish and five loaves that they wanted to make Jesus king—by acclamation! (Luke 9:10-17; John 6:1-15). Especially during His time in Galilee, Jesus was a popular leader.

Luke's Portrait of Jesus

2. A Powerful Leader

One of the things that motivated people to follow Jesus was His demonstration of God's power—both in His teaching and His miraculous healings. They said He spoke "with authority" (Luke 4:32). The way the Jewish rabbis taught was first to make a statement and then support it with quotes from various authoritative sources. Jesus spoke like the Old Testaments prophets. They didn't do a lot of quoting to establish the correctness of what they said. Their authority was based on the fact that they were God's spokespersons. They often prefaced their statements with "thus saith the Lord." What other authority was needed?

Jesus' authority rested on His relationship to God and on the power of God with which He worked miracles. A good example is His healing of "Mr. Paralee" (5:17-26). Jesus said, "so that you will know I have authority to forgive sin, I'll enable this man to walk." Jesus spoke and the man walked. That's power. At another time, a Roman officer requested that Jewish leaders ask Jesus to heal His servant. When Jesus got close to the house, the officer said, "Jesus you don't have to come in my house. You're a man of power. Just speak the healing word and my servant will be well." Jesus spoke the word and His servant got well (7:1-10). That's power!

One more example. This time Jesus was sleeping in a boat out on the Sea of Galilee when a storm came up. When they finally woke up Jesus because they thought they were going under, Jesus got up and spoke to the wind and water and "there was a great calm" (8:22-25). That's power!

3. A Wise Leader

One of the wonderful things about Jesus is that He was not selfish with His power. When the right time came, He "called [His] disciples together and gave them power" also (9:1). Now they too could exercise the power of God to heal the sick, drive out demons and preach the Gospel.

One of the slogans Jesus teaches us not to repeat is: "If you want something done right, do it yourself." Jesus teaches us this principle: *If you want something done right, first do it yourself and then teach someone else how to do it.* Jesus didn't send the disciples out to preach or

Jesus: Man With a Following

heal the sick or cast out demons until He had done it first. After letting them observe Him, then He sent them out to do it on their own—without Him watching over their shoulders. Apparently they did well (9:6). On the next mission, He added more personnel and they did well also (10:1-12, 17-20).

Another important lesson that Jesus teaches us is that developing effective leadership takes much time. The exercise of power was rather easy, but they also had to learn when *not* to exercise power (9:51-56), how to pray (11:1-13), the proper attitude toward negative influences (12:1-3), fear (12:4-7) persecution (12:8-12), material possessions (12:13-21) and how to trust God for their daily needs (12:22-34). Jesus spent many hours patiently teaching His potential leaders before He finally released them to go into all the world. They were effective because they had been well taught and equipped and were now Spirit-filled (Acts 1:4-8; 2:1-18).

4. A Compassionate Leader

In Luke 5, verses 12-16 Luke tells the story of a leper ("Mr. Lep") whom Jesus healed with a touch. Leprosy was such a terrible disease that ordinary people didn't want to be anywhere near a leper. But in this story "Jesus reached out and touched him" (5:13). Why? Mark tells us that Jesus was "moved with compassion" (Mark 1:41, KJV). In chapter 9, verses 10-17, Luke recounts the miracle of the two fish and five loaves with which Jesus fed 5,000 hungry men as well as women and children. Jesus and His disciples were very tired and were trying to get away for some rest.

He had told His disciples to come and "rest a while." But here were these thousands of people looking for healing and help. He interrupted His plans in order to minister to them. Why? He was "moved with compassion toward them" (6:34, KJV).

Jesus was just coming down from a tremendous "high" that He had experienced on Transfiguration Mountain (Luke 9:28-36). Up there the "Godness" that He usually kept hidden broke out and even His clothes glowed with released divinity. Moses and Elijah came for the occasion and God Himself spoke out of the clouds. But at the foot of the mountain was a father with a boy who was being taken advantage of by demons. Yes, he had a bad case of epilepsy—only worse. (The devil does not cause all of our problems but he always makes them worse.) Jesus seemed a little upset that the disciples were not able to drive out the demon and heal the boy. Jesus finally said, "Bring the boy to me." He drove out the evil spirit and gave the boy back to his father. Why? The boy's father put his finger on Jesus' motivation. He said, Jesus, "have compassion on us, and help us" (Mark 9:22, KJV).

Read the stories of "Sister Bentover" (Luke 13:10-17), "Brother Dropsy" (14:1-16), His concern for the people of Jerusalem (13:31-35; 19:41-44), the stories of the lost sheep and the Prodigal Son (15:1-7, 11-32) and see if you come away with the same sense of concern, empathy, and compassion. Jesus loved people, and it showed in His attitude and actions. He was a compassionate leader.

5. A Challenging Leader

Yes, Jesus was popular, powerful, and wise. He was also compassionate, especially to the sick, helpless, and hopeless; but He was also challenging, particularly to those who wanted to participate with Him in ministry—or thought they did.

After telling His disciples that He was going to be put to death, He challenged them to be prepared to take up their cross also (9:21-26). Later in the same chapter, He challenged them to greatness through service (9:46-48), the toughness of forgiveness (9:51-56) and the discipline of singlemindedess (9:57-62).

In chapter 14, Jesus lifted up the challenge of humility and concern for the poor (14:7-24), of giving God priority, counting the cost of discipleship (14:25-33) and remaining "salty" by maintaining consistent Christian character (14:34-35). In chapter 15, the disciples are challenged to have a positive attitude, and to take positive action to save the lost, and in chapter 16, to evaluate their perspective toward material possessions.

The disciples' biggest challenge was understanding and being faithful to Jesus during the last days of His life on earth. This challenge they

Jesus: Man With a Following

failed miserably. Mark tells us (Mark 14:50, KJV), "they all forsook him, and fled."

6. A Suffering Leader

On at least three occasions, Jesus told His disciples that He was going to suffer and die (Luke 9:21-22, 44-45; 18:31-33). But even after the third time "they did not understand any of these things, the meaning of the words was hidden from them, and they did not know what Jesus was talking about" (18:34). Isn't that something? What was the problem?

One of the problems was history. Much of Jewish history is the story of bondage—bondage in Egypt, bondage in Babylon and bondage in Palestine, their own country. You see, Jews are Jews because of their relationship to God, Jehovah, Yahweh. As long as they are faithful to God, God protects them and provides for them. When they are unfaithful to God, they are at the mercy of their strongest neighbors. Like most of humanity, the Jews are usually in a state of unfaithfulness and therefore in a condition of bondage or approaching bondage. In this state they are looking for a deliverer—someone whom God will use to help bring them back into a right relationship with God and free them from their bondage.

Some of their great deliverers were Moses, Joshua, Gideon, Deborah, David and Hezekiah. It was during David's reign as king that they experienced their Golden Age, and so they often viewed their deliverer as a "Son of David" (18:38-39). Another title for this deliverer is "Messiah" in Hebrew or "Christ" in Greek. So in a sense, the history of Israel is the story of the anticipation and coming of deliverers or messiahs. Their picture of a Messiah was a leader that was popular, powerful, wise and compassionate like Jesus. And so some of the disciples and other Jews were convinced that Jesus was truly the Messiah (2:23-32; 9:20; John 6:15).

The problem was also contemporary. At the time when Jesus was on earth, the Jews in Palestine were under the rule of the Romans. In fact, in 70 A.D., 40 or so years after Jesus' ascension, the Romans destroyed Jerusalem as Jesus prophesied in Luke 19:41-44; 21:5-24. The Jews were under bondage again and looking for a Messiah to deliver them.

Luke's Portrait of Jesus

Some of them thought that Jesus was their Messiah and He was—but He was not a political Messiah. He was a spiritual Messiah, a suffering Messiah; the One described in Isaiah 53:

> ISAIAH 53:1 The people reply, "Who would have believed what we now report? Who could have seen the Lord's hand in this?
>
> 2 It was the will of the Lord that his servant grow like a plant taking root in dry ground. He had no dignity or beauty to make us take notice of him. There was nothing attractive about him, nothing that would draw us to him.
>
> 3 We despised him and rejected him; he endured suffering and pain. No one would even look at him—we ignored him as if he were nothing.
>
> 4 "But he endured the suffering that should have been ours, the pain that we should have borne. All the while we thought that his suffering was punishment sent by God.
>
> 5 But because of our sins he was wounded, beaten because of the evil we did. We are healed by the punishment he suffered, made whole by the blows he received.
>
> 6 All of us were like sheep that were lost, each of us going his own way. But the Lord made the punishment fall on him, the punishment all of us deserved.
>
> 7 "He was treated harshly, but endured it humbly; he never said a word. Like a lamb about to be slaughtered, like a sheep about to be sheared, he never said a word.
>
> 8 He was arrested and sentenced and led off to die, and no one cared about his fate. He was put to death for the sins of our people.

Jesus: Man With a Following

> 9 He was placed in a grave with evil men, he was buried with the rich, even though he had never committed a crime or ever told a lie." 10 The Lord says, "It was my will that he should suffer; his death was a sacrifice to bring forgiveness. And so he will see his descendants; he will live a long life, and through him my purpose will succeed. 11 After a life of suffering, he will again have joy; he will know that he did not suffer in vain. My devoted servant, with whom I am pleased, will bear the punishment of many and for his sake I will forgive them. 12 And so I will give him a place of honor, a place among great and powerful men. He willingly gave his life and shared the fate of evil men. He took the place of many sinners and prayed that they might be forgiven." (TEV)

That's why Jesus told the disciples He was going to suffer, die and rise again. And because they were looking for a conqueror, not a sufferer, they couldn't comprehend what Jesus was talking about—and never did—until after the Resurrection.

Actually, we can understand the disciples' dilemma. We African Americans are a suffering people. We came here in bondage and have been in bondage ever since. That's why Martin Luther King, Jr. was such a dilemma for many of our people and why Malcolm X had a greater appeal—especially to the less spiritual and unchurched. King came talking about love and suffering. Malcolm came talking self-defense and force. They were two of our African American "Messiahs." And we discovered what all who look to messiahs discover. Messiahs do not deliver. God delivers in response to, and to the extent of, our faithfulness to Him. True liberation is first of all spiritual. Ultimately the extent of our freedom is the extent to which we bring our spirits in harmony with His. Could this be why the disciples never understood or

Luke's Portrait of Jesus

experienced real liberation until after they had a spiritual experience on the Day of Pentecost? It was then that the Comforter came and began to teach them all things and to bring back to their memories the things that Jesus had said to them (John 14:26). With their newfound freedom, they were able to go into all the world and free others.

Yes, Jesus was a Man with a following. They didn't understand where He was leading them, but they followed for various reasons and those who followed to the end were set free.

7

Jesus: Man With a Mission

In four separate passages of Luke, Jesus expresses His mission (4:18-21, 43; 5:32; 19:10). Jesus made the most extensive expression of His mission near the beginning of His ministry in His hometown of Nazareth. Jesus had recently completed a solitary retreat in the desert where He spent 40 days in prayer, meditation and fasting. A part of His meditation time had been spent battling with the forces of evil that were seeking to derail His ministry by having Him fall into the traps of materialism, compromise or sensationalism. He resisted these temptations by knowing and obeying the Scriptures—the Word of God (4:1-13). Then after a time of ministry in Galilee, He went home and went to church as was His habit (4:14-16).

The manager or president of the synagogue handed Him a scroll (there were no books as we know them in those days) of Isaiah. He unrolled the scroll to Isaiah 61 and read from it. (Luke 4:18-19)

He finished reading, gave it back to the attendant, sat down and said: "This passage of scripture has come true today, as you heard it being read" (4:21, TEV). Jesus had stated His mission:

1. To bring Good News to the poor
2. To proclaim freedom to the bound
3. To bring health to the sick
4. To announce deliverance to God's people

The second statement of Jesus' mission is in Luke 4:43. He is in Capernaum now, has gone to church again and there driven an evil spirit out of a man (4:31-37), healed the mother of Peter's wife of a high fever (4:38), and healed numerous people who had gathered outside the

Luke's Portrait of Jesus

house after the sun had already gone down (4:39-41). At daybreak Jesus got up and tried to get away for some time alone. But wouldn't you know it, they came and found Him and "tried to keep him from leaving" (4:42)! It was then that Jesus reiterated a central part of His mission. He said:

> "I must preach the Good News
> of the Kingdom of God
> in other towns also,
> because that is what God
> sent me to do" (4:43, TEV).

Jesus made the third statement of His mission in Luke 5:32. Since His second statement, He had already called four of His 12 disciples (5:1-11), and healed two men—"Mr. Lep" (5:12-16) and "Mr. Paralee" (5:17-26). After Levi or Matthew accepted his call as the fifth disciple, he gave a big party to celebrate his new relationship with Jesus, and he invited some of his friends from the "IRS" and others of his not–so–respectable buddies. Some of the Pharisees and their associates passed by just when the party was in full swing and were appalled to see Jesus right in the middle of things. They called some of Jesus' disciples over and said, loud enough for Jesus to hear: "Why are you–all eating with 'those folk?' They are low–life tax collectors and sinners!" (5:30)

Jesus did not argue with them about their character assessment of His new friends. He used this opportunity to restate His mission:

> "People who are well
> do not need a doctor,
> but only those who are sick.
> I have not come
> to call respectable people
> to repent, but outcasts" (5:31-32).

The story of another tax collector is the setting for a final restatement of Jesus' mission (19:1-10). "Brother Zack" (Zacchaeus) had several problems: 1) He, like Matthew, was a collector of taxes for the Roman government, the oppressors of his people, the Jews—which in a sense made him a collaborator with the enemy. So on a scale of 1–10, his

Jesus: Man With a Mission

popularity was probably a minus 10. 2) He was rich. He was not only a hated tax collector, but he was also a "chief" and had gotten rich in the process of extracting taxes from his people for the enemy. 3) He was short, so he was probably pushed around wherever he walked in public and was the butt of many "short people" jokes. As he walked down the street he heard someone ask: "Who in the Bible was shorter than Zacchaeus?" Answer: "Bildad, the shoe-height" (Job 25:1). And so the jokes would go as various "respectable" Jews tried to hurt Brother Zack in whatever way they could.

But Brother Zack had one great desire—he wanted to see Jesus. And today as Jesus was on His way to Jerusalem through Jericho, his wish would be fulfilled. You can read the whole story in Luke 19:1-10. But what happened is that Jesus invited Himself to Brother Zack's house for dinner and as usual the "respectable" people complained. Zacchaeus repented of his sins and promised to make restitutions. Jesus took the opportunity to restate His mission:

"The Son of Man came to seek
and to save the lost" (19:10).

As we look at these four statements, can we say that Jesus' mission was to those who need health, help and hope? To the sick, the diseased, the disabled and demon possessed, He brought health. To the poor, the weak, the guilty and outcasts, He brought help. To the disappointed, dispossessed, disillusioned, defeated and desperate, He brought hope. The subjects of Jesus' ministry were those who needed help and knew it.

Can we say secondly that the *condition* for receiving Jesus' ministry was repentance? The word "repent" means to make a 180 degree turn and go in an opposite direction. In our context, repentance symbolizes a willingness to admit a personal need and to meet the necessary requirements to receive the benefits. The New Testament records very few Pharisees, Sadducees, scribes or lawyers who received healing, health or hope from Jesus. They were not willing to fulfill the conditions to receive the healing, help and hope that Jesus offered.

Can we say thirdly that the *power* for Jesus' ministry came from God? "The Spirit of the Lord is upon me," He read in Nazareth (4:18) and "that is what God sent me to do," He said in Capernaum (4:43).

Luke's Portrait of Jesus

Jesus was not the source of His own power. Jesus knew at the beginning of His ministry, what some people seem never to discover—the power to do ministry is not of us or *from* us; it is *through* us. Jesus knew the source of His power and therefore never "ran out" of power. He could be absolutely worn out, so tired physically that He could sleep through a storm. But if you woke Him up He could calm the raging sea. Exciting? Yes! And that same power for ministry is available to us.

In summary, Jesus' mission was to employ the power of God to bring health, help and hope to people who were willing to admit their need and meet the requirements for their deliverance.

8

Jesus: Man of Effective Methods

How did Jesus carry out His mission? That's the question we want to explore in this chapter. Matthew helps us with his two summaries of Jesus' ministry.

"And Jesus went about all Galilee, teaching in their synagogues, and preaching the gospel of the kingdom, and healing all manner of sickness and all manner of disease among the people" (Matthew 4:23, KJV).

"And Jesus went about all the cities and villages, teaching in their synagogues, and preaching the gospel of the kingdom, and healing every sickness and every disease among the people" (9:35, KJV).

Jesus' mission was to minister health, help and hope to those who were willing to admit their need and meet the requirements for their deliverance. The methods by which Jesus accomplished this mission were teaching, preaching and healing. Let's look at each method separately. In this chapter we'll look at Jesus as Preacher and Healer, and in the following chapter as Teacher.

1. Preaching

A first way that Jesus carried out His mission was by preaching or proclaiming the Gospel, the Good News about the kingdom. It is difficult to make a definitive distinction between Jesus' preaching and teaching. In fact, in Luke's account Jesus Himself does not seem to make such a clear distinction. But both in Luke 4:18-19 and 4:43, He clearly stated He was chosen and sent by God to preach. And though He was considered during His ministry and is considered now to be one of history's most effective teachers, these texts from Luke seem to indicate

Luke's Portrait of Jesus

that He might have preferred to be thought of as a preacher. Perhaps some of the best examples of His preaching in Luke are: 4:18-27; 6:20-49; 11:37-54; 11:1-12, 22-40, 49-50; as well as 13:1-15; 14:25-35 and 17:1-4. In those passages we find these characteristics:

1. The proclamation is monological rather than dialogical.

2. The proclamation is declarative and imperative rather than indicative and inquisitive.

3. The proclamation demands clear choices and decisive action.

4. The proclamation promises rewards and punishment for choices made and action taken.

5. The proclamation is not simply truth declared but also truth applied.

6. The proclamation was addressed to groups, usually large groups rather than individuals.

7. The proclamation usually involved a focus on the character and action of God–Father, Son or Holy Spirit.

Preaching was one of the methods Jesus used to carry out His mission of bringing people health, help and hope.

2. Healing

A second way that Jesus carried out His mission was by healing. Luke's healing stories may be divided into at least five categories: 1) curing sicknesses, diseases and disabilities, 2) casting out demons and evil spirits, 3) a combination of "curing and casting," 4) forgiving sins, 5) restoring the dead to life.

A. Jesus healed bodies—Jesus' statement of purpose in Luke 4:18, included "recovery of sight to the blind" (TEV). His actions indicate that His concern for the blind was symbolic of His anointing to minister to persons with all kinds of physical ailments. In fact, Luke only records the healing of one blind person (18:35-43), but he records the healing of Peter's mother–in–law who had a "high fever" (4:38-39), one man (5:12-16) and ten men (17:11-19) who had leprosy, a woman with a blood disease (8:42-48), and a man with dropsy or severely swollen legs

Jesus: Man of Effective Methods

and arms (14:1-6). Besides these specific cases of individual healing, Luke records that on some occasions Jesus healed everybody present who was sick (4:40; 6:19; 9:11).

B. Jesus healed minds—In addition to healing physical ailments and afflictions, Jesus also healed people who had mental and emotional illnesses by casting from them demons and evil spirits. Luke records only three cases. The first was in a synagogue in Capernaum (4:31-37), the second was in a graveyard (8:26-39), and the third was at the foot of Transfiguration Mountain (9:37-43). Jesus might have referred to His intention of casting out demons in His phrase, "to set free the oppressed" (4:18).

C. Jesus healed minds and bodies—A third category is the healing of those who had both physical and emotional illnesses. Such persons were the "many people" included in Luke's reports in 4:40-41 and 6:17-19, but especially "Sister Bentover" who was not only bent over physically but had a "spirit of infirmity" (KJV) that Satan had used to keep her in bonds for "eighteen years" (13:10-17). Then one day Jesus came to her church and told her that she was free from her sickness. She then straightened up and praised God.

Free at last
Free at last
Thank God Almighty
I'm free at last!

D. Jesus healed spirits—There were those whom Jesus gave a spiritual healing, the forgiveness of their sins. The first man is "Brother Paralee" whom Jesus forgave and healed (5:17-26). The second person was the prostitute who was in love with Jesus and Jesus knew it. He said, "She loved much" (7:47, KJV). She embarrassed Simon the Pharisee with her display of affection, but Jesus told her that her sins were forgiven and to go in peace (7:36-50). What a beautiful story. What a wonderful Saviour.

The other two spiritual healings were of Zacchaeus, the rich "IRS" man (19:1-10) and the thief on the cross (23:40-43). In neither case is the word "forgiveness" used, but the aroma of forgiveness is present. You sense that the One who seeks and saves the lost, does it by forgiving their sins.

E. Jesus raised the dead—Finally Jesus healed those smitten by death. In the Gospels there are three such cases. Luke records the stories of two of them: the son of "Sister Nain" (7:11-17), and the daughter of "Brother Jarius" (8:40-42, 49-56). Only John records the story of Brother Lazarus (11:1-45). There is some controversy surrounding the story of Jarius's daughter. The argument is about whether she actually was dead as the messenger from Jarius's house announced and the people at the house believed, or whether she was "only sleeping" as Jesus said. We have put her in the category of those whom Jesus "healed from death." But if Jesus had the power to bring her back to life, doesn't it make sense that He would know whether or not she was dead?

Curing sick people, casting out demons, forgiving sins and restoring people to life were all parts of Jesus' healing ministry. His healing ministry gave many people new health, help and hope, and brought many people who came to see the miracles under the influence of His preaching and teaching.

9

Jesus, The Teacher

Jesus carried out His ministry not only by preaching and healing but also by teaching. Teaching is the science and art of communicating ideas and skills. Teaching is a science because all effective teaching follows certain principles. It is an art because of the individual ways in which these principles are applied. Teaching communicates ideas—products of the mind—thoughts, facts and concepts; and skills or actions of the body such as writing, typing, playing basketball, driving a car and playing the piano. Both ideas and skills are communicated through teaching and Jesus was a master communicator.

Like all effective teachers, Jesus used a variety of teaching methods. Here is a list of some of the methods He used most frequently which are described in the Gospel of Luke:

1. Question and Answer or Discussion
2. Parables and Stories
3. Sayings
4. Lectures
5. Demonstrations

1. Question and Answer or Discussion

As can be seen from its position on our list and can be confirmed by a reading of Luke, the method that Luke records as used most by Jesus was the discussion or question and answer method. A list of places in the Book of Luke where Jesus used this method is rather long, but seven

Luke's Portrait of Jesus

examples can be found in chapters nine and twenty alone. Perhaps the most well-known question and answer session is this expanded conversation which Jesus had with His disciples (9:18-20):

Jesus: Who do people say that I am?
Disciple 1: Some say you are John, the Baptist.
Disciple 2: Yes, and others say you are Elijah.
Disciple 3: Other people don't know but...
Disciple 4: They think you're one of the other prophets...
Disciple 5: Somebody come back to life.
Jesus: Really? Is that what they say?
Disciples in unison: Yes, they're saying all kinds of things.
Jesus: How about you all? Who you think I am? (long pause)
Peter: We think you're the Christ, the anointed One, God's Messiah.

Luke was not present and ends his version of the conversation with Peter's declaration. Matthew was there and gives a fuller version of the conversation in Matthew 16:13-20. Both Matthew and Luke record that Jesus followed up the discussion with a brief lecture on His coming death and resurrection, and the cost of discipleship (16:21; Luke 9:21-27). Jesus loved the discussion method of teaching and used it extensively.

2. Parables and Stories

The second of Jesus' "most used methods" and the method for which He is best known, especially as presented by Luke, is the parable and storytelling method. All parables are not stories and all stories are not parables. But many of Jesus' parables are stories and for our purposes we are including them in the same category. Perhaps a basic difference between a story and a parable is that a parable always involves comparison. The word "parable" is derived from a Greek word which means "to throw beside" or "to compare."[29] A story may be written or told simply to communicate facts, feelings and/or skills, or just to entertain. A biblical parable is told to help the listener decide between options and to act on the basis of his/her decision. When Jesus finished telling the story of the Good Samaritan (10:25-37), He asked the lawyer, "In your

Jesus, the Teacher

opinion, which one of these three acted like a neighbor toward the man attacked by the robbers?" (10:36) The lawyer had to make a decision based not only on the information he heard in the parable but also on a comparison with the values he had been taught. The lawyer replied that the man who acted like a neighbor was "The one who was kind" to the man who was robbed (10:37). Then Jesus said, "You go, then, and do the same." In essence, Jesus said, "You see your options, choose one and act on it!" When Jesus used parables as a teaching method, He expected three things: hearing, deciding and acting.

The study of Jesus' parables is a fascinating one. For further study, three books are *must* reading: *Parables of the Kingdom* by C.H. Dodd, *Interpreting the Parables* by Archibald M. Hunter and *The Parables of Jesus* by Neal F. Fisher.

3. Sayings

A saying by Jesus was usually a one or two sentence summary of a principle that was stated so well that once you heard it, it was difficult to forget it. For instance: "People who are well do not need a doctor, but only those who are sick" (5:31). Or, "Happy are those who hear the word of God and obey it" (11:28). Or, "Salt is good, but if it loses its saltiness, there is no way to make it salty again" (14:34). Or, "It is easier for heaven and earth to disappear than for the smallest detail of the Law to be done away" (16:17). Perhaps Jesus' most memorable sayings in Luke are those He spoke from the cross:

"Father, forgive them; for they know not what they do" (23:34, KJV).
"Today shalt thou be with me in paradise" (23:43, KJV).
"Father, into thy hands I commend my spirit" (23:46, KJV).

Jesus' sayings, as with most one or two sentence summaries—such as "a stitch in time saves nine," or "nothing succeeds like success" or "if at first you don't succeed, try and try again"— are not designed to stand alone. They are usually the culmination or "punch line" to what has already been taught or the introductory sentence for a lesson to come.

Jesus usually used these sayings as summaries to nail down a point and make it easily recallable in the minds of His listeners.

4. Lectures

As stated in the discussion of Jesus' preaching, it is sometimes difficult to make a definitive distinction between Jesus' teaching and preaching, particularly between His preaching and lecturing. However, it is possible to demonstrate Jesus' use of the lecture method when giving information and instructions to His disciples on specific topics and when seeking to impart understanding about Himself.

A. *Jesus lectured to His disciples*—Here are some examples of Jesus' lectures: 10:2-16; 11:1-13; 14:7-14; 18:31-34; 21:5-28; 24:25-32; 24:45-49.

In each of the lectures that we have identified, Jesus is conversing with His disciples. Jesus usually spoke to the crowds in parables (8:9-10; Matthew 13:34), but in at least these seven instances in Luke, He spoke to His disciples in monologues on specific topics.

B. *Jesus lectured on specific topics*—In Luke 10:2-16, Jesus instructed His disciples how to conduct themselves when on an evangelistic mission. In 11:1-13, He taught them how to pray and in 14:7-14, He taught them how to act when they went to a wedding. In 18:31-34, He told them what to expect when they arrived in Jerusalem and in 21:5-28, He informed them about some of the events that would happen after His ascension. In 24:25-27, 45-49, He tried to help them understand Him in relation to Old Testament prophecies.

Lectures were not Jesus' usual way of teaching, but when He perceived that an extended monologue was the most effective way of imparting urgently needed information or instructions quickly, He used it.

5. Demonstrations

Jesus not only taught by using discussion, sayings, parables, stories and lectures, He also taught by *demonstrating* the truth He wished to com-

Jesus, the Teacher

municate. In a sense, His whole life was a demonstration of His relationship to God and people. In a deeper sense, His life was a demonstration of what God intended for us to be and the manner in which we are to conduct our earthly lives. But as an effective teacher, Jesus demonstrated some practical, everyday lessons He wished to teach. Let's look at a few examples.

A. The "Church" Habit—Jesus wanted to teach the habit of assembling with the people of God. So He established a personal habit of going to the synagogue.

4:15 "...He taught in the synagogues..."

4:16 "...he went as usual to the synagogue."

4:32 "...he spoke with authority. In the synagogue..."

4:44 "So he preached in the synagogues..."

6:6 "On another Sabbath Jesus went into a synagogue..."

13:10 "One Sabbath Jesus was teaching in a synagogue."

Jesus was consistent in attending synagogue services, especially during the early and middle parts of His ministry (chapters 4--13). His acceptance at the synagogues was not uniform. Sometimes the people praised Him (4:15, 36), at other times the Jewish leaders tried to trap Him and wanted to kill Him (6:7, 11), but until fierce persecution and the size of His audience made it less possible, Jesus demonstrated the importance of going to church by His habitual attendance at synagogue services.

B. The Prayer Habit—By praying habitually Jesus taught His disciples and others the importance of prayer.

3:21 "Jesus also was baptized. While he was praying, heaven was opened."

5:16 "But he would go away to lonely places, where he prayed."

6:12 "At that time Jesus went up a hill to pray and spent the whole night there praying to God."

9:18 "One day when Jesus was praying alone, the disciples came to

Luke's Portrait of Jesus

him. 'Who do the crowds say I am?' he asked them."

9:29 "While he was praying, his face changed its appearance, and his clothes became dazzling white."

11:1 "One day Jesus was praying in a certain place. When he had finished, one of his disciples said to him, 'Lord, teach us to pray...'"

Isn't that interesting? Jesus was a great miracle worker, a great healer and a preacher. But the only thing that Luke records that the disciples asked Jesus to teach them, was how to pray. Could it be that they recognized the connection between Jesus' prayer life, His staying in touch with His Father, and His teaching–preaching–healing–miracle-working power? Could it be that they concluded that if they could learn how to pray, then the teaching–preaching–healing–miracle–working power would be theirs? Sounds right, doesn't it?

Jesus knew it was extremely important that the disciples learn to pray, and so in addition to lecturing on prayer (Matthew 6:5-15; Luke 11:1-13), and telling parables about prayer (18:1-8, 9-14), He modeled prayer and demonstrated in His life the importance and power of praying habitually (see also 22:41-42; 23:34-36).

C. The Scripture Habit—Nowhere in Luke are the disciples or the crowds told that Scripture is important and that they should read and memorize it. Of course, people didn't have easy access to the Scriptures as we do now. There were no Bibles in book form then. The Old Testament Scriptures were written by hand on scrolls or rolls of paper–like material that were kept in the synagogues and the temple. These scrolls were brought out at a certain time in the service, read to the congregation, commented on and put away until the next service.

So Jesus did not tell His disciples and others to read and study the Scriptures, but He demonstrated in His life the importance of knowing and doing the Scripture. Because Luke was writing primarily for non–Jewish readers, he did not quote extensively from the Old Testament. Matthew did, because he was writing for Jews who were familiar with the Scriptures. However, Luke gives ample evidence that Jesus knew the Scriptures and believed they were important. For instance, during

Jesus, the Teacher

His temptations, He quoted from the Scriptures: "It is written..." at least one time for each temptation (4:4, 8, 12, KJV). When teaching on the Sabbath (6:3-4) and when preparing to heal "Brother Witherly" (6:9), He referred to the Scriptures. When defending John the Baptist (7:27), He quoted the Scriptures and later declared that true happiness was/is experienced by "those who hear the word of God and obey it" (11:28). Some of His favorite Old Testament characters were: Abraham (13:16; 16:22, 23, 27, 29-31; 19:9; 20:37), Moses (9:30; 16:16, 31; 20:37; 24:27, 44) and David (6:3; 20:41-44). He read from Isaiah (4:17) and referred to Elijah (4:25-26; 9:30), Elisha (4:27), Jonah (11:29, 32), Solomon (11:31; 12:27), Lot (17:29) and Isaac and Jacob (20:37). Jesus also referred to the Ten Commandments, the Law (14:3; 16:16; 18:19-21) and the Scriptures (19:46; 20:17; 21:22).

The exciting highlight of Jesus' love for the Scriptures and His anointing to interpret them was climaxed on His journey to Emmaus. There, He explained to His companions, "what was said about himself in all the Scriptures, beginning with the books of Moses and the writings of all the prophets" (24:27). Later that evening He opened His disciples' minds to understand the Scriptures and said to them, "This is what is written: the Messiah must suffer and must rise from death three days later, and in his name the message about repentance and the forgiveness of sins must be preached to all nations, beginning in Jerusalem" (24:45-47).

By demonstration, Jesus taught the value and authority of the Scriptures. They are ours to read, study, meditate on, live and share.

D. *The Love Habit*—What is the one word that best summarizes Jesus' life? Did you say love? Yes, and yet as we read Luke, how little we hear Jesus *talking* about it. Then how can we conclude that love was so important to Jesus? He demonstrated it! Love is the essence of His life. Its aroma rises from every page. Love is why He healed people (5:12-16), forgave people (7:37-50; 23:34), accepted people (19:1-10), fed people (9:10-17) and raised people back to life (7:11-16). Jesus loved people. He didn't talk about it all the time, but He demonstrated it in His every act. The supreme demonstration was when He gave His life

Luke's Portrait of Jesus

on Calvary. John recognized the demonstration and interpreted it in the Scriptures' most well-known verse:

> "For God so loved the world,
> that he gave his only begotten Son,
> that whosoever believeth in him
> should not perish,
> but have everlasting life"
> (John 3:16, KJV).

A modern song writer recognized Jesus' demonstration, and asked the question and then gave the answer:

> Why should He love me so?
> Why should He love me so?
> Why should my Saviour to Calvary go?
> Because He loved me so.[30]

God's love through Jesus Christ is just as powerful and available today as it was the day of Jesus' death. Anyone who is willing to admit their need, can believe it, receive it and experience a wonderful change in their lives TODAY (John 1:11-12; 2 Corinthians 5:17).

6. Summary

Jesus was a teacher who used various methods to communicate His Good News. Whether He used discussion, sayings, parables, stories, lectures or demonstration, it is clear that He loves us and came to bring healing, help and hope into our lives.

PART III

JESUS, OUR EXAMPLE

As you have already discovered, this book is divided into three main parts. In part one we looked at Luke, the author and Luke, the Gospel account. Part two centered around Luke's portrait of Jesus and this final section is built on four statements of faith:

1. Jesus is not only our Saviour and Lord, He is also our Example. Peter reminds us that Christ left us an *example* so that we can *follow in His steps* (1 Peter 2:21).

2. Jesus' life is composed of a series of critical experiences, beginning at His birth and leading to His resurrection and ascension.

3. These critical experiences are our sign posts—pointing the way to spiritual maturity and effective Christian ministry.

4. As followers of Jesus Christ, we can expect that some, if not all, of these critical experiences will be repeated in our lives somewhere along our Christian journey.

Therefore, let us identify and examine some of Jesus' experiences to see what lessons we can learn to help us on our journey. In Chapter Ten we will follow Jesus from Bethlehem to Nazareth, and in Chapter Eleven we will trace His journey from Galilee to Bethany.

10

Experiences: Bethlehem to Nazareth

1. Bethlehem: An Experience of Poverty

>Away in a manger
>No crib for a bed,
>The little Lord Jesus
>Laid down His sweet head;
>The stars in the heavens
>Looked down where He lay,
>The little Lord Jesus
>Asleep on the hay.[31]

The words and especially the tune of this Christmas song are so beautiful that they mask the discomfort, pain and embarrassment of this poverty experience. Imagine how Mary and Joseph must have felt. The angel had told them almost a year before that they were going to be parents to the Son of God. And now all that they could provide for Him was a stable, an animal feeding trough, and some rags for a blanket.

Three–fourths of the world lives in poverty. To *live* in poverty means the experience of "making do."

>It means being born wherever and
>whenever nature says it's time.
>It means eating what you can
>When you can.
>It means "making do."

Luke's Portrait of Jesus

> It means wearing what you have,
> No matter what the occasion.
> It means not having what you need
> But using what you have.
> It means "making do."

"Making do" is not always pleasant but it is a valuable experience. It teaches us how to create "soul food" out of what's left of the master's pig and to feed 5,000 men with two fish and five bagels (Luke 9:13-14). It teaches us how to make beautiful dresses out of flour sacks and to create eye salve from mouth juice and dirt (John 9:6). It teaches us how to make musical drums out of barrels and how to make a donkey the leader of a royal procession (Luke 19:35-38).

We should not romanticize poverty. We should try to extricate ourselves from it and help other people out of it. Poverty is not to be either despised or clung to. It is an experience, we should learn from it and move on. Jesus was born in Bethlehem, but it was not His permanent home.

2. Jerusalem: A Learning Experience

Luke records that Jesus went to Jerusalem three times: once as a baby (1:22-38), once as a teen (2:41-52), and as a an adult near the end of His life (19:45-46). It is the second experience that we would like to focus on.

A. *It's wonderful to have caring parents*—Everybody is not so blessed, but it's wonderful to have parents who love and care for you. And to them, you really never grow up. When Mary and Joseph found out Jesus was not with their caravan they were "terribly worried" (2:48), as if He were six or seven years old. They made a "bee line" back to Jerusalem and finally found Him in the temple (2:46). To them, He was still their little boy. Luke said, Mary "treasured up all these things…in her heart" (2:19, NIV). Is it possible that Jesus allowed all of their concern, care and love to go unnoticed?

Experience: Bethlehem to Nazareth

B. It's wonderful to be exposed to stimulating teachers—When they found Jesus, He was basking in the glow of appreciative teachers. Luke said, He was "sitting with the Jewish teachers, listening to them and asking questions. All who heard him were amazed at his intelligent answers" (2:46-47). Next to salvation, there is nothing as important as education. Blessed is the person who loves knowledge and seeks understanding. Blessed are the persons who seek the company of those from whom they can learn and share serious thoughts and skills.

"Birds of a feather flock together."
"If you fool with trash,
It will get in your eyes."
"If you lay down with dogs
You'll rise up with fleas."
"If you hang with the wise
It's hard to become a fool."

Jesus increased in wisdom (2:52) because He kept company with the wise.

C. Church is wonderful—When Mary asked Jesus, "Why have you done this to us?" Jesus answered in 12–year–old fashion, with His own question: "But Mom, why did you all have to look for Me? Didn't you know that I would be in my Father's house (or place of business)?" Jesus loved church. When He was outside of Jerusalem, He made a "habit" of going to the synagogue (4:16), and when He came to Jerusalem, He went to the temple, sometimes "every day" (19:47).

Jesus found that there was something uniquely wonderful about the church experience. It cannot be experienced at home, at school, at the supermarket or bank. There is a Spirit, an indescribable positive presence that adds quality to everyday living. Having had a genuine worship experience, we feel added to, we feel more than we were before, we know that we are an integral part of a larger reality. (See Isaiah 6:1-8 for a better description!) Church is wonderful. Those who know its value, go often.

Luke's Portrait of Jesus

D. Obedience is valuable—There's a strange verse of Scripture in Hebrews 5:8. Speaking of Jesus, it says, "Though he were a Son, yet learned he obedience by things which he suffered" (KJV). The suffering does not apply to Luke 2:51 but there is a connection of some kind in the "learning obedience" part. This occasion did not teach Jesus to obey His parents. But from this experience the value of obedience is confirmed. Luke 2:52 is dependent upon verse 51. Had Jesus not "went back with [His parents] to Nazareth, where he was obedient to them," He could not have grown into a fully and positively developed young man—physically, mentally, spiritually and socially. By obedience to our parents, we learn the value of respect for order and authority in other areas of life. Yes, He was Jesus, the divine Son of God but He obeyed His parents and grew up to be the Person about whom God could say:

> "You are my dear Son;
> I love You and
> I am pleased with You"
> (Luke 3:22, paraphrased).

3. Jordan: An Experience of Identification

That phrase, "You are my dear Son…" is also a translation of the words Jesus heard "from heaven" when He was baptized in the Jordan River (3:21-22). It was an occasion of great drama. Jesus must have told the story. John said he saw the Spirit come down upon Jesus symbolized by a dove, but it seems that only Jesus heard the voice of God (John 1:32-34; Luke 3:22).

Why all the drama? Why the baptism, the dove and the voice?

A. The Baptism represented Jesus' identification with John —John was a peculiar person in many ways. He lived in the desert. He ate grasshoppers and honey.[32] He looked like an ancient Tarzan with his camel hair clothes and big leather belt. His speech was rough, pointed and anything but diplomatic.

He called the Jewish leaders snakes and compared them to rotten trees that God was getting ready to cut down and burn (see Matthew

Experience: Bethlehem to Nazareth

3:1-10). John was a tough character. But he was "the best thing going." John and Jesus were in harmony in their understanding of God and His kingdom and their commitment to doing God's will. So Jesus ignored all of John's outward peculiarities and through baptism, identified Himself with John's message and ministry.

B. The dove was God's way of identifying Jesus to John—Even though they were cousins (Luke 1:36), it seems that they had never met as adults, because John did not know who Jesus was and certainly did not know He was the Messiah. John said, "I saw the Spirit come down like a dove from heaven and stay on him. I still did not know that he was the one, but God, who sent me to baptize with water, had said to me, 'You will see the Spirit come down and stay on a man; he is the one who baptizes with the Holy Spirit.' I have seen it," said John, "and I tell you that he is the Son of God" (John 1:32-34).

C. The voice was God's way of identifying Himself with Jesus and perhaps identifying Jesus to Jesus as the Messiah—We're moving here in the realm of mystery. We really don't know what experience of intimacy was occurring between Father and Son. But we know that Jesus was getting ready to begin His public ministry, a ministry *to* the suffering and a ministry *of* suffering, a ministry that involved obstacles, intense opposition and eventually death. As God, He is completely secure, but as man, He needed the assurance that He was doing what pleased God. So God spoke "out of heaven" and told Him: "Yes, Jesus, You are who You believe You are. You are My special Son, My dear Son. I love You and I am pleased with what You're doing" (Luke 3:22, paraphrased).

D. It seems that Jesus' baptism models for us three requirements for entering effective ministry—1) We should not try to be original or try to be the Lone Ranger but should identify with an ongoing ministry. Shouldn't there be someone to whom the Lord is speaking that harmonizes with what the Lord is saying to us and through us—maybe not exactly in method, but in essence? We should be very hesitant, if we're the only one. Remember the poem by John Donne?

Luke's Portrait of Jesus

> No man is an island
> No man stands alone,
> Each man's joy is joy to me
> Each man's grief is my own;
> *We need one another,*
> So I will defend
> Each man as my brother,
> Each man as my friend.[33]

Even if you believe you can make it alone, don't try. Ask the Lord to identify someone to you and identify you to someone. John needed Jesus and Jesus needed John.

2) Don't go into ministry without divine approval. We often speak of *our* ministry of preaching, teaching, singing, healing and so on. But actually we have no ministry. All ministries are God's ministries that we do as His instruments. Our identification and approval experience may not be as dramatic as Jesus'. It may come in a private moment, late at night—the still small voice—or it may come at the end of a high moment of public worship (Isaiah 6:1-8). When it comes, you will know it. Expect it. Prayerfully wait for it (Luke 3:21). It will come.

4. The Wilderness: An Experience of Decision

After Jesus' baptism, He "was led by the Spirit into the desert, where he was tempted [or tested] by the Devil" (Luke 4:1-2). Jesus knew His *mission*. It was to minister, to serve those who need health, help and hope, and then to give His life (Mark 10:45), but how should He accomplish His mission? What would be His *methods*? The devil had three suggestions. Can you imagine this conversation?

Devil: Offer the people bread.

Jesus: Bread?

Devil: Yes, something that they can touch, taste and smell. Give them something *material*.

Jesus: All right. I'll consider that but let Me see what God says.

God: Man cannot live on bread alone.

Experience: Bethlehem to Nazareth

Jesus: Bread is good but it is not enough.

Devil: Then offer the people a *compromise.*

Jesus: A compromise?

Devil: Yes, don't make them choose between You and me, between good and evil. Let them have both at the same time.

Jesus: How do you propose to do that?

Devil: Well, if You worship me by giving me Your approval, and I worship You by giving You all of my power and wealth, then people won't have to decide between us. They can have the best of both worlds.

Jesus: Really?

Devil: Really. Then people can just do what they want to. Sin and guilt will be eradicated. There will be no need for God. It will just be me and You.

Jesus: All right, I'll consider it. A world in which there is no conflict between good and evil is an appealing idea.

Devil: Very appealing.

Jesus: Yes, but let's see what God says.

God: I alone am to be worshiped and served. I am the Creator of all human beings, therefore their original allegiance is to Me. They can be satisfied and totally happy only when they choose to worship and serve Me exclusively.

Devil: I have a third suggestion.

Jesus: What is it? So far you're batting zero.

Devil: Show the people something *spectacular.*

Jesus: Something spectacular?

Devil: Yes, their lives are so dull—home, work; work, home; home, work, church; home, work, school; home...

Jesus: I get the picture. What do you have in mind?

Devil: Something really big. Something like jumping off the temple.

Jesus: Are you crazy?

Devil: It would add some excitement to people's dull, dreary lives—home, work; work...

Luke's Portrait of Jesus

Jesus: I know...I told you I get the picture. But who's going to jump off the temple?

Devil: You!

Jesus: Me?

Devil: The Lord promised, He promised to send angels. You won't get hurt.

Jesus: You are a fool.

Devil: No, hear me out. I can see it now. You jump and the sky is suddenly filled with angels. With my connections, ABC, CBS, NBC, CNN and even PBS will be there to give You international coverage. You'll be the talk of the world. They'll make You the world leader...

Jesus: Satan...

Devil: People will come to You from all over the world.

> No tedious walking over hot sand.
> No stormy travel by boat
> No frustrating arguments
> with Jewish leaders.

Jesus: Satan...

Devil: No endless teaching and healing and preaching with nobody really understanding what You're talking about.

Jesus: SATAN!

Devil: No being beaten and spit on, denied, betrayed, forsaken and crucified.

Jesus: Okay, okay, okay, I'll consider it, but let's see what God says.

God: Jesus, You know what Your mission is and You know My plan to achieve it.

Jesus: But Father...

God: Now Son, don't test Me to see if I will accommodate Your human nature and the devil by going against My own will.

Devil: Well, I guess that's it for now.

Jesus: Yes, you've wasted enough of My time. Now get out of here.

Experience: Bethlehem to Nazareth

Devil: I'm gone...but I'll be back.

What is the meaning of this imaginative presentation of Jesus' wilderness experience?

1. Never consider yourself beyond temptation. As Jesus was tested, everybody who follows Him can expect to be tested also. "The Tempter" is one of the devil's titles and testing folk is a part of his SOP (Standard Operating Procedure).

2. Expect the devil to test you at what he perceives to be your weakest time.

3. The devil's suggestions will sound rational, will appeal to the comfort of our bodies, our temporary emotional security, and will be designed to help us think we can avoid suffering.

4. Our most effective defense is our knowledge of and appeal to God's Word.

5. The devil's end to our test is temporary. Someone has said, "Never think that you have rebuked the devil for the last time."

5. Nazareth: The Experience of Rejection

The experience of rejection is an important part of the maturing process. When Jesus left the wilderness, He went back to Galilee. He was full of physical and spiritual energy. He was a young and gifted teacher "and was praised by everyone" (Luke 4:15).

That is, *until* He went back home to Nazareth where He had grown from childhood to manhood, from a carpenter's son to a carpenter, from a student to a teacher. The word had gotten back about how well He was doing and how God was blessing His ministry. So they asked Him to be guest preacher for the Sabbath service. He chose Isaiah 61 as His text.

"The Spirit of the Lord is upon me, because he has chosen me to bring good news to the poor. He has sent me to proclaim liberty to the captives and recovery of sight to the blind, to set free the oppressed and announce that the time has come when the Lord will save his people" (Luke 4:18, 19, TEV).

When He finished reading the Scripture, He announced, "This passage of scripture has come true today, as you heard it being read" (4:21).

At first they were favorably impressed. In fact, they didn't get too bothered with His comments about their expectations and a prophet not being welcomed in his hometown. But when He said that His interest and God's interest were not only in Jewish poor, and Jewish captive, and Jewish blind and oppressed, but also in Gentiles whom they abhorred and despised and counted as dogs and worse—when He said that, they "went off."

They grabbed Him, dragged Him out of town and "meant to throw him over the cliff" (4:29). What are the lessons of the Nazareth experience?

1) Do not go around expecting everybody to reject you. Many people will love you and accept you (4:14-15).

2. Be prepared to be rejected by those who have known you longest and best. It may not happen, but prepared for it.

3. Make sure your message and ministry have a firm scriptural foundation (4:18-19).

4. Do not allow people's acceptance or rejection to determine whether or not you carry out your God-given assignment.

5. The Christian message is universal. Do not proclaim it as if its boundaries are sectarian, denominational, racial or ethnic.

6. Don't stay around and allow people to kill you before your time (4:30). Go on to "Capernaum;" your ministry may be welcomed there (4:40).

11

Experiences: Galilee to Bethany

1. Galilee: An Experience of Popularity

Where was Galilee?

The word "Galilee" comes from a Hebrew word meaning "circle" which kind of describes Galilee's geography.[34] The area was circular, extending westward toward the Mediterranean Sea, bordered by Phoenicia on the West and North, on the East by the Jordan River and on the South by Samaria and the Ten Towns (Decapolis).

In size, Galilee was about 50 miles from north to south and 25 miles from east to west. It was rather densely populated, containing about 204 villages, "none with less than 15,000" people, having a total population of about 3,000,000 folks. The land was fertile, the climate pleasant and the people courageous and open–minded but also volatile and hot–tempered.[35]

Luke recorded that in Galilee, Jesus chose, trained and sent out His disciples (5:1-11, 27-32; 6:12-16; 9:1-6), announced the Beatitudes and kingdom principles (6:20-49) and raised two young people back to life (7:11-17; 8:40-42, 48-56). It was also in Galilee that Jesus forgave a prostitute (7:36-50), accepted women "disciples" (8:1-3), and told His famous parable of the seed and sower (8:4-15). There, He also spoke peace to a storm (8:22-25), fed 5,000 men, plus women and children (9:10-17), disclosed that He was the Messiah (9:18-20), experienced a transfiguration (9:28-36) and began to speak of His death and resurrection (9:21-27, 43-45). In Galilee He also healed many sick and demon possessed people (4:38-41; 5:12-26; 6:6-11, 17-19).

Jesus was very popular in Galilee. Phrases such as these are found in this section of Luke's report:

Luke's Portrait of Jesus

"The people were all amazed...And the report about Jesus spread everywhere in that region" (4:36-37).

"After sunset all who had friends who were sick with various diseases brought them to Jesus; he placed his hands on every one of them and healed them all" (4:40).

"The people started looking for him, and when they found him, they tried to keep him from leaving" (4:42).

"He preached in the synagogues throughout the country" (4:44).

"...The people pushed their way up to him to listen to the word of God" (5:1).

"...The news about Jesus spread all the more widely, and crowds of people came to hear him and be healed from their diseases" (5:15).

"And [Herod] kept trying to see Jesus" (9:9).

"All the people were amazed at the mighty power of God" (9:43).

So what shall we say about the popularity experience?

A. Rejection in one place, does not mean rejection in every place. Mark records that Jesus was not able to perform any miracles in Nazareth, except that He placed His hands on a few sick people and healed them (Mark 6:5). Had Jesus accepted that as the measure of His ministry, He would have surely considered Himself ineffective. But He knew Nazareth didn't represent all of Galilee. In other parts of Galilee He healed people "by the droves" (Luke 4:40-41).

B. People respond to a variety of ministries and ministers. Jesus offered people healing for their bodies, teaching for their minds and souls, forgiveness for their guilt, health and restoration for their children, opportunities for partnership ministry, and on at least one occasion in Luke, food for their hunger (9:10-17). If we meet people's felt needs, we can expect a flourishing ministry.

C. Don't try to do ministry alone, recruit and train assistants.

Experience: Galilee to Bethany

D. Accept people's appreciation and compliments, but keep your attention on doing God's will. Twice during His time of popularity, Jesus told His disciples that He had to go to Jerusalem to suffer, die and be raised again to life (9:21-27, 43-45). "But the disciples did not know what this meant" (9:45). This brings us to our next point.

E. Do not expect even your closest associates to understand your vision. Tell it to them. Remind them of it, as Jesus did. But do not be disappointed if they do not understand. Luke explained that Jesus' meaning "had been hidden from them so that they could not understand it..." (9:45). In his most famous book, *The Prophet*, Kahlil Gibran said:[36]
> "The vision of one man
> lends not its wings to another man."

F. The popularity experience will not last indefinitely. Popularity depends on crowds and crowds are very fickle. When you stop giving them what they want when they want it, they are likely to turn on you (Luke 11:14-15) or turn away *from* you (John 6:66). Take advantage of the popularity period to do as much good as possible, because it is a period of limited duration.

2. The Hill of Transfiguration: An Experience of Preparation

Why did Jesus go up to Transfiguration Mountain and take three of His disciples with Him? Was it just for the drama? It's an exciting story—the glowing face, the clothes turning a brilliant white, the presence of Elijah and Moses, Peter's suggestion and the voice from heaven! WOW! But what did it mean? It was a time of preparation for Jesus' experiences in Jerusalem and His ministry of suffering. Not just suffering but the *ministry* of suffering.

A. The ministry of suffering means suffering that we experience so that someone else will not have to suffer. Much of our suffering is deserved and self–imposed. Suffering as a *ministry* is suffering, voluntarily accepted for the benefit of someone else. It's an intense type of suffering that needs to be prepared for.

Luke's Portrait of Jesus

B. Preparation for the ministry of suffering requires prayer. "And [Jesus] went up a hill to pray" (Luke 9:28). Prayer prepares us to do the difficult by bringing our human nature under the control of the divine nature and bringing our human will in harmony with God's will (11:2; Matthew 6:10). Prayer prepares us to suffer.

C. Preparation for the ministry of suffering requires confirmation. "Suddenly two men...Moses and Elijah...appeared in heavenly glory and talked with Jesus about the way in which he would soon fulfill God's purposes by dying in Jerusalem" (Luke 9:30-31). Not just anyone can help you prepare for suffering. Those most helpful are those who have been through the experience. Moses and Elijah qualified. They had experienced the ministry of suffering and were now experiencing "heavenly glory" (9:31). So God pulled them out of retirement and told them in effect "Go down and help prepare my Son for His ministry of suffering."

If you're suffering or preparing to suffer, don't suffer alone. Ask the Lord to send you somebody to assist you.

D. Expect that those closest to you may not be of much assistance to you. "Peter and his companions were sound asleep..." (9:32). There is a spiritual that says:

> You must walk this lonesome valley,
> You've got to walk it by yourself.
> O nobody else can walk it for you,
> You've got to walk it by yourself—
> You've got to walk it by yourself.

Should you have the companionship of a spouse, a relative or friend, count yourself extremely blessed, but be prepared for those close to you to sleep through the experience.

E. Finally, expect to hear the Voice. It may be a verse of Scripture, the line of a poem or hymn, a vision in the night, or the refrain of a sermon.

Experience: Galilee to Bethany

But just as surely as you listen, you will hear the Voice. And the Voice will speak words of love and encouragement. Listen for the Voice.

3. Jerusalem III: The Experience of Suffering

Beginning with chapter nine, verse 51, Luke starts his record of Jesus' journey to Jerusalem. And almost immediately we began to see Him being rejected, opposed and otherwise persecuted. In 9:51-56, He is refused hospitality in a Samaritan village, and in 57-62, various people give Him excuses for not following Him. In 10:13-16, He pronounces judgment upon three prominent Galilean cities that have not responded to His message of repentance. In 11:14-23, some people accuse Him of using Beelzebub's (Satan's) power to cast out demons, and in 11:29-32, the crowd demands a miracle. Luke records Jesus' denunciation of the Pharisees and lawyers in 11:37-54, and in 11:1-12, He warns His disciples about hypocrisy and fear, and warns others of the danger of speaking against the Holy Spirit.

On His journey to Jerusalem, Jesus heals a few people (13:10-17; 14:1-6; 18:35-43)—often in spite of the opposition of the Jewish leaders or over the protest of an unsympathetic crowd. And Luke retells some of Jesus most famous stories, often aimed at the sins of the rich and powerful (12:13-21; 14-15-24; 16:1-13, 19-31; 18:1-8, 18-30), or the prejudices of a Jewish crowd (15:1-32). It is no longer popular to be Jesus. It is His time of opposition. How does He teach us to handle it?

A. Expect it. Jesus did not expect His wave of popularity to last indefinitely. When He told the story of "Mr. Sand" and "Mr. Stone" (6:46-49), He predicted that some would hear His word and not obey it. When He told the parable of the seed and soil, He predicted that only a fourth of the seed would fall into good soil and bear fruit (8:4-15). When He sent out the disciples, He had them understand that they would go into towns where people wouldn't welcome them (9:5), and as He started His journey toward Jerusalem, He warned His disciples, that "whoever rejects you rejects me; and whoever rejects me rejects the one who sent me" (10:16). Rejection did not take Him by surprise. He expected it. The pastor of a fast growing church, speaking at a pastor's

Luke's Portrait of Jesus

conference said: "If you present a plan and nobody opposes it, don't do it. If the plan is from God, somebody will oppose it!" Expect opposition. If it hasn't come yet, be thankful and careful. It's on the way!

B. Prepare for it. During the journey to Jerusalem, Jesus spent much time teaching His disciples—teaching them how to handle rejection (9:51-62), how to do evangelism (10:1-12), how to handle success (10:17-20), how to deal with prejudice (10:25-37), how to pray (11:1-13; 18:1-8), how to handle false accusations (11:14-23) and persecution (11:4-12), and how to trust God to supply their needs (12:22-34; 18:28-30). His purpose was to get them ready to carry on after His ascension by preparing them to face fierce opposition and persecution in an unfriendly world. He said, "when (not if) they bring you to trial in the synagogues or before governors or rulers..." Jesus knew His followers would face intense suffering. He tried His best to prepare them for it—by giving them His words, teaching them to pray and giving them some "hands–on" experience in practical ministry.

Once Jesus arrived in Jerusalem, there was a brief celebration, now known as Palm Sunday (19:37-40), and from that point the opposition and persecution continued in a downward spiral. The forces of evil would not be satisfied except by the taste of blood. And so on Good Friday, they killed Him. He had already accepted this as the path to which His life was leading. After forgiving His enemies (23:34) and saving a dying thief (23:43), He put His life into the hands of the One who gave it to Him, breathed His last breath and died (24:46).

C. Accept it. Accept the fact that suffering is a part of Christ–like living and serving. Paul, Luke's mentor said, "For you have been given the privilege of serving Christ, not only by believing in him, but also by suffering for him" (Philippians 1:29). Peter, probably one of Luke's research sources declared, "...if you endure suffering even when you have done right, God will bless you for it. It was to this that God called you, for Christ himself suffered for you and left you an example, so that you would follow in his steps" (1 Peter 2:20-21). The symbol of Christianity is not a Cadillac, BMW or Mercedes Benz; it is not a big bank

Experience: Galilee to Bethany

account, an expensive house or a wall full of degrees. The symbol of the Christ–like life is the Cross.

>Must Jesus bear the Cross alone,
>And all the world go free?
>No, there's a Cross for everyone,
>And there's a Cross for me.[37]

D. Understand that suffering is temporary.

>"I'm so glad trouble don't last always," therefore:
>The consecrated cross I'll bear,
>Till death shall set me free,
>And then go home my crown to wear,
>For there's a crown for me.[38]

4. Resurrection/Ascension: The Experience of Victory

Life can be described by many symbols. It can be viewed as a school where each experience is a lesson; or as a body where each experience represents growth; or, it may be seen as a painting where every experience is a brush stroke moving the picture toward completion; or as a symphony where every experience is a note urging the composition toward fulfillment. But to many, life is a war, and each experience a battle to be won or lost. One of the church's favorite songs of past generations was "Onward Christian Soldiers," where under Paul's inspiration (Ephesians 6:10-17), the church was pictured as a mighty army.[39] Although Luke does very little editorializing (he just tells the story), underneath the facts, the battle is apparent to those who are perceptive.

There was a battle between Jesus and the Jewish leaders (Luke 22:1-6, 47-53, 66-71). There was a battle between the Jewish leaders and Pilate (23:1-6, 13-25) and between the Jewish leaders and Herod (23:7-12). There was conflict within Peter, between who he was and who he wanted to be (22:31-34, 54-62). There was a conflict within Judas, between who Jesus wanted him to become and who he became (22:3-6, 47-48). There had already been a conflict between the two

Luke's Portrait of Jesus

thieves condemned to die with Jesus (23:32-43). And above, beneath and around all these events was the war raging between Satan and God. On Good Friday, God apparently lost—Jesus was condemned to death, tortured, crucified and buried (23:13-56).

It was a happy day for the devil and the forces of evil. Did they have a victory party in hell that night? Did they have a ticker tape parade down the streets of the Inferno to celebrate the death of God's Son? Didn't they know that their victory was temporary? Didn't they know that God seldom loses a battle and never loses a war? Hadn't Satan told his demons about the Garden of Eden? Moses in Egypt? Or Joshua at Jericho? Hadn't they read about Deborah and Sisera? Gideon and the Midianites? Or David and Goliath? Well, both the unknowing forces of evil and the unbelieving good people were in for a big surprise. Because God always has the last word and that word is good.

> Luke 24:1 Very early on Sunday morning the women went to the tomb, carrying the spices they had prepared.
>
> 2 They found the stone rolled away from the entrance to the tomb,
>
> 3 so they went in; but they did not find the body of the Lord Jesus.
>
> 4 They stood there puzzled about this, when suddenly two men in bright shining clothes stood by them.
>
> 5 Full of fear, the women bowed down to the ground, as the men said to them, "Why are you looking among the dead for one who is alive?
>
> 6 He is not here; he has been raised. Remember what he said to you while he was in Galilee:
>
> 7 The Son of Man must be handed over to sinful men, be crucified, and three days later rise to life.'"

Experience: Galilee to Bethany

8 Then the women remembered his words. (TEV)

Later, Jesus appeared to some of His folk on the road to Emmaus and afterward to His other disciples, to explain to them the relationship between Old Testament prophecy and New Testament victory and to show them the physical evidence that He was really alive and had victory over death and the grave (24:13-16). What He had earlier told them to keep secret, He now told them to announce everywhere—after they went back to Jerusalem and received the Holy Spirit's anointing (24:47-49). About six weeks after Easter, He took them to Bethany, blessed them and ascended back to heaven (24:50-51). The disciples worshiped Him and went back to Jerusalem to begin a victory celebration that is still going on (24:52-53).

Luke ends his story on a note of victory!

NOTES

INTRODUCTION
1. William Barclay, *The Gospel of Luke* (Philadelphia: Westminster, 1975), pp. 1-5.

2. Herbert Lockyer, *All the Men of the Bible* (Grand Rapids: Zondervan, 1958), p. 220.

3. William Martin, "Luke," *Layman's Bible Encyclopedia* (1964), p. 482.

LUKE, THE WRITER
4. G.B. Caird, *Saint Luke* (Philadelphia: Westminster, 1963), p. 16.

5. Albert Barnes, "The Gospels," *Barnes' Notes on the New Testament* (Grand Rapids: Baker Book House, reprinted from the 1884-85 edition), p. iii.

6. For more information on the "we" passages, see: Donald Miller, "Luke," *Layman's Bible Commentary,* vol. 18 (1982), p. 24; Donald Juel, *Luke–Acts: The Promise of History* (Atlanta: John Knox Press, 1983), p. 6.

7. Caird, p. 16.

8. *Ibid.,* p. 17.

9. Barnes, p. 1. See also Caird, p. 15; Miller, p. 25; and Barclay, p. 1.

10. Barnes, p. 1.

11. Caird, p. 15.

12. Barclay, p. 1.

13. I. Howard Marshall, *Luke: Historian and Theologian* (Grand Rapids: Zondervan, 1971 edition), p. 25.

14. Barclay, pp. 1-2.

LUKE, "THE GOSPEL"
15. For other interesting comments on Theophilus, see Caird, p. 44.

16. R.A.T. Murphy, "Luke, Evangelist, Saint," *New Catholic Encyclopedia* (1967), p. 1071. See also Juel, p. 4 and Marshall, pp. 57-67.

17. Miller, p. 10.

18. Reginald Fuller, "Luke, Gospel According to St.," *Encyclopedia*

Americana (1989), p. 842.

19. See: Juel, p. 8 and Murphy, p. 1070.

20. Words and music by Gloria and William Gaither, "Because He Lives," *The Worshiping Church, A Hymnal* (Carol Stream, IL: Hope Publishing Company, 1990), p. 238.

FREEDOM: THE CENTRAL MESSAGE

21. "How Firm a Foundation" (verse 2), *The Worshiping Church*, p. 612.

22. "O for a Thousand Tongues to Sing" (verse 3), *The Worshiping Church*, p. 130.

MAJOR THEMES

23. See: Juel, p. 104; see also Barclay, p. 3.

24. Barclay, p. 4.

25. See: Jaroslav J. Pelikan, "Christianity," *Encyclopedia Britannica*, vol. 5 (1967), p. 693.

LUKE'S PORTRAIT OF JESUS

26. Barclay, p. 1.

27. *Ibid.*

JESUS: MAN WITH A FOLLOWING

28. These words were spoken by Dr. O.T. Jones, Jr., at a minister's conference in Philadelphia, PA.

JESUS, THE TEACHER

29. Neal Fisher, *The Parables of Jesus* (New York: Crossroads, 1990), p. 24.

30. Unknown source.

EXPERIENCES: BETHLEHEM TO NAZARETH

31. The words are by an anonymous poet. The music to the most frequently sung tune was arranged by James R. Murray. The "Cradle Song" tune was written by William J. Kirkpatrick. See: "Away in a Manger," *The Worshiping Church: A Hymnal,* pp. 147 and 148.

32. Locusts have two identities, one as grasshoppers and the other as

a fruit that grows on wild trees. "Grasshoppers" was chosen because it seems in harmony with John's personality.

33. These more modern words are adapted from an old English poem by John Donne.

EXPERIENCES: GALILEE TO BETHANY

34. Barclay, p. 45.

35. *Ibid.*

36. Kahlil Gibran, *The Prophet* (New York: Knopf, 1983 edition), p. 63.

37. "Must Jesus Bear the Cross Alone," words by Charles Wesley, music by Lowell Mason. *The Worshiping Church: A Hymnal* (1st verse), p. 658.

38. *Ibid.* (2nd verse).

39. "Onward Christian Soldiers," words by Sabine Baring-Gould, music by Arthur S. Sullivan. *The Worshiping Church: A Hymnal*, p. 748.

SOURCES AND RESOURCES

Barclay, William. *The Gospel of Luke.* Philadelphia: Westminster, 1975.

Barnes, Albert. "The Gospels," *Barnes' Notes on the New Testament.* Grand Rapids: Baker Book House, reprinted from the 1884-85 edition.

Caird, G.B. *Saint Luke.* Philadelphia: Westminster, 1963.

Danker, Frederick. *Luke, Proclamation Commentaries.* Philadelphia: Fortress, 1976.

Fisher, Neal. *The Parables of Jesus.* New York: Crossroads, 1990.

Fitzmeyer, Joseph. "The Gospel According to St. Luke," *Anchor Bible.* Vol. 28, 1981.

Fuller, Reginald. "Luke, Gospel According to St.," *Encyclopedia Americana.* Vol. 17, 1989, p. 842.

Hobbs, Herschel. *Luke–Good News for All People.* Nashville: Convention Press, 1980.

Juel, Donald. *Luke–Acts: The Promise of History.* Atlanta: John Knox, 1983.

Lockyer, Herbert. *All the Men of the Bible.* Grand Rapids: Zondervan, 1958.

Lockyer, Herbert. *All the Parables of the Bible.* Grand Rapids: Zondervan, 1963.

Marshall, I. Howard. *Luke: Historian and Theologian.* Grand Rapids: Zondervan, 1971 edition.

Martin, William. "Luke," *Layman's Bible Encyclopedia.* Vol. 3, 1964, p. 482.

Miller, Donald. "Luke 18," *Layman's Bible Commentary.* 1982.

Murphy, R.A.T. "Luke, Evangelist, Saint," *New Catholic Encyclopedia.* 1967, p. 1071.

Richards, Larry. *U-Turn: Dr. Luke's Guide to a New You.* Wheaton, IL: Victor Books, 1973.

Taylor, V. "Luke, Gospel of," *The Interpreter's Dictionary of the Bible.* Vol. 3, 1962.